2/n

Thomas Alva Edison

Thomas Alva Edison

INVENTOR AND ENTREPRENEUR

CLAIRE PRICE-GROFF

FRANKLIN WATTS
A Division of Scholastic Inc.
New York Toronto London Auckland Sydney
Mexico City New Delhi Hong Kong
Danbury, Connecticut

Photographs © 2003: Brown Brothers: cover, 2, 18, 76; Corbis Images: 14, 102 (Bettmann), 25 (Hulton-Deutsch Collection), 6 (Museum of the City of New York), 71, 82, 112 (Schenectady Museum, Hall of Electrical History Foundation), 110 (Underwood & Underwood), 56; Edison National Historic Site, National Park Service, US Department of the Interior: 10 left, 10 right, 11, 35, 36, 42, 47, 48, 52, 80, 88, 90, 99 bottom, 104; From the Collections of Henry Ford Museum & Greenfield Village: 8, 59; Nick Romanenko: back cover, 13, 21, 27, 50, 54, 73, 91, 92, 99 top; North Wind Picture Archives: 23; Smithsonian Institution, Washington, DC/National Museum of American History, Electricity Collection: 38, 62, 109; Thomas A. Edison Papers, Rutgers University: 30.

Library of Congress Cataloging-in-Publication Data

Price-Groff, Claire.
   Thomas Alva Edison : inventor and entrepreneur / by Claire Price-Groff.
     p. cm. — (Great life stories)

Summary: Explores the life of Thomas Alva Edison, the inventor of numerous devices, including the light bulb and the phonograph.

Includes bibliographical references and index.
   ISBN 0-531-12275-1

1. Edison, Thomas A. (Thomas Alva), 1847-1931—Juvenile literature. 2. Inventors—United States—Biography—Juvenile literature. 3. Electric engineers—United States—Biography—Juvenile literature. [1. Edison, Thomas A. (Thomas Alva), 1847–1931. 2. Inventors. 3. Scientists.] I. Title. II. Series.

TK140.E3P72 2003
621.3'092—dc21

2003000956

Contents

Before the age of railroads and electricity, life was slow paced.

ONE

Always Curious

Imagine a world without electric lights. When the sun goes down, the only light outdoors comes from the stars and the moon. Homes are lit by flickering gas or oil lamps. People travel on foot, or by horse and wagon, stagecoach, or boat. The only way to send news to a distant family member was by mail, which can take weeks or even months to be delivered.

By the 1830s, railroad trains chugging along gleaming tracks made travel faster and easier. News tapped out in Morse code sped instantly from one city to another through telegraph wires.

Neither railroads nor telegraphs had reached the small town of Milan, Ohio, on February 11, 1847, when Samuel and Nancy Edison's seventh child, Thomas Alva, was born. They called him by his middle name, perhaps to honor Samuel's old friend for whom the child had been named. Little

Alva had a tiny body and a large head. The doctor who delivered him warned that he might not survive. His parents, fourteen-, eighteen-, and two-year-old sisters, and sixteen-year-old brother hoped the doctor was wrong, especially since two other children in the family had died within the past few years. Luckily, as winter turned to spring, Alva grew stronger. His overly large head seemingly contained a normal, healthy brain.

The Edisons, who had come to the United States from Canada, lived in Milan, Ohio, where Samuel ran a small business milling lumber and making roof shingles. At that time, Milan, located on a canal that linked it to the Great Lakes, and through them to the rest of the country, was one of the most important wheat-shipping ports in the Midwest. The Edison family prospered along with the rest of the town's residents.

The rapid spread of the railroads ended this prosperity. As more goods were transported on trains than on canal boats, Milan lost its place as a major shipping port. Samuel's business declined, and when Alva was seven years old, the family moved to Port Huron, Michigan, where there was more opportunity.

By this time, Alva's sisters were both married with families of their

Even as a young child, Thomas Alva was full of curiosity.

own (his third sister had died months after Alva's birth), and his brother no longer lived at home, leaving Alva to be raised as an only child. Shortly after the move, he contracted scarlet fever, which left him prone to respiratory and ear infections. It also affected his hearing. When Alva was well, he tagged along with his father to pick up lumber or run other errands about town. Besides his lumber business, Sam Edison also engaged in other enterprises. He was an easygoing man who was always eager to try new things. When one thing didn't work out, he shrugged his shoulders and went on to try something else. His son grew up to be very much the same way.

A DIFFICULT PUPIL

Port Huron had no public school, so when Alva was eight years old, his parents enrolled him in Reverend George Engle's private school. Reverend Engle, like most teachers of the time, expected his students to learn by memorizing lists of facts. Students were expected to sit quietly and listen to their teachers. Questions and curiosity were discouraged. Students who fidgeted too much or did not pay attention felt the sharp sting of a switch. Alva did not do well in this setting. He asked lots of questions and stared out the window. He often did not hear the teacher and found it difficult to pay attention.

Many of Edison's biographers have written that after only a few months at this school, his mother withdrew him and taught him at home. As an adult, Edison said that his mother did this because Reverend Engle said he was easily confused and unable to learn. This may have been part of the reason his mother removed him from school, but the more likely reason was that his parents could no longer afford the $130 annual tuition. Nancy had been a teacher before she married and felt she was qualified to home-school her son. She also may have been concerned about his frail health.

Unlike her husband, a nonbeliever who seldom attended church, Nancy was very religious. She sent her son to both church and Sunday school. She also used the Bible as one of her basic teaching tools, along with the many different kinds of books in her husband's extensive home library.

One result of Alva's homeschooling was the development a lifelong love of reading. "My mother taught me how to read good books," he said,

Edison credited his mother Nancy Elliot (left) with imparting to him his love of reading and learning and his father Samuel Edison (right) with his sense of adventure and insatiable curiosity.

"and as this opened up a great world in literature, I have always been very thankful for this early training."

However, Reverend Engle's school was not the only one Alva attended. In 1859, when he was eleven years old, he attended the recently opened, one-room Port Huron public school, perhaps because his mother felt ill equipped to instruct him in science. It was at this school that Alva was introduced to *A School Compendium of Natural and Experimental Philosophy*, a book that had a profound influence on him. Using the book's instructions for conducting simple experiments, he set up his first laboratory in his parents' basement. Books could "show the theory of things," but "doing the thing itself is what counts," he often said.

A YOUNG ENTREPRENEUR

Few youngsters at that time attended school beyond the eighth grade. Alva was no different. When he was twelve years old, he decided he had had enough schooling. He wanted to work so he could help improve his family's worsening financial situation. He knew just what job he wanted—one on the Grand Trunk Railroad, a Canadian line that had recently established a depot in Port Huron on its route to Detroit.

Alva didn't exactly work for the railroad. He went into business for himself as a "candy butcher," selling magazines, newspapers, candy, and tobacco to passengers on the daily train to Detroit. He showed his initiative and entrepreneurial ambition by selling vegetables from his father's garden as well as other items.

His job was not an easy one. The train left Port Huron early in the morning, arrived in Detroit a few hours later, and then left Detroit for the return trip late in the afternoon. Alva made good use of his time in Detroit, which was a large, bustling city, a major port on the Great Lakes, and an industrial and shipping hub for the entire country. He joined the Detroit Young Men's Society and spent many hours reading books in its extensive library. He also enjoyed exploring the dock area and busy city streets where he scrounged around machine shops, book stores, and chemists to find materials to use in his lab, which he had relocated from his house to a corner of the train's baggage car.

His baggage-car lab came to an inglorious end when a bottle of phosphorus fell off a shelf and ignited. Some of Edison's biographers say that after the fire was put out, the train's conductor boxed Alva's ears so badly he could no longer hear, and that his deafness stemmed from this incident. However, a different story states that another time, Alva was late for the train and was lifted aboard by his ears. Edison later told people, "I felt something snap inside my head, and my deafness started from that time and has ever since progressed." Most likely, neither of these stories is completely true. Both may have occurred, but Alva's deafness had been increasing steadily since the time he had scarlet fever as a young child.

Alva brought his chemicals home, reestablished his lab in his parents' basement, and conducted his experiments late at night. As this left him more free time on the train, he purchased a second-hand press, used type, ink, and other supplies. He then used the baggage car as a press room in which to publish his own newspaper, the *Grand Trunk Herald*.

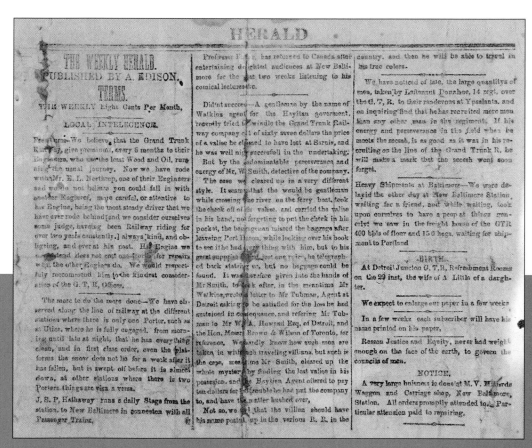

In this edition of his newspaper, *The Grand Trunk Herald*, Edison wrote editorials praising the work of his favorite engineer and a hard-working porter at one of the train depots. He also wrote a story about a man who tried to swindle the railroad with a false claim of lost luggage and one about the numbers of men recently recruited for service in the Civil War.

This was quite an industrious endeavor for a fifteen-year-old boy. He gathered the news, wrote the stories, set the type, ran the press, and sold the papers.

He quickly discovered that doing all the work himself was too much, so after a few issues he hired his friend William Wright, who had worked as a printer's helper in Port Huron. The two boys began a new paper, *Paul's Pry*, which they published for a few months in 1862. This venture ended when Alva wrote a gossipy story about a local doctor's son, and the doctor threatened to dunk the writer in the river. Alva decided that publishing papers was too risky and went back to selling the *Detroit Free Press*.

A NEW INTEREST

During the three years he worked on the train, Alva enjoyed visiting with the telegraph operators at the stations between Port Huron and Detroit. He had seen a continual increase in telegraph traffic and knew it would continue. This

This is page from the patent for telegraph signs by Samuel Morse. This system of signs is known as Morse code.

prompted his decision to become a telegraph operator. He taught himself Morse code on a simple telegraph set he had made and arranged his schedule so he could spend more time at the Mt. Clemens station where his father's friend, James MacKenzie, was the telegraph operator.

One day, Alva saw MacKenzie's three-year-old son playing on the railroad tracks. He also saw a freight train zooming around the bend. Alva hurled himself onto the tracks, clasped the boy to his chest, and rolled out of the way.

MacKenzie was so grateful to Alva for saving his son's life that he agreed to teach him telegraphy. Alva hired someone to replace him on the train while it traveled between Mt. Clemens and Detroit so he could have more time for his lessons. At home, he strung wires between his and a friend's house, a half mile away, and practiced with his homemade set.

It may have been around this time that Alva's father introduced him to the writings of Thomas Paine, one of the Founding Fathers of the United States, who is most well known for his pamphlet "Common Sense," which helped rally the colonists to fight against the British. The book that particularly influenced both young Alva and his father was Paine's *Age of Reason*.

In this book, Paine questioned commonly held beliefs about religion and philosophy. Paine felt that natural law and science, not Biblical revelation, was the path to true knowledge. This reasoning appealed to Alva, just as it did to his father.

Much later, Edison said, "I can still remember the flash of enlightenment which shone from his [Paine's] pages. It was a revelation, indeed, to encounter his views on political and religious matters, so different from the views of many people around us. . . ." Alva felt he had found someone he could use as a life model—especially when he discovered that Paine had been an inventor as well as a revolutionary and a philosopher. Alva took Paine's words, "under all discouragements, [man] pursues his object, and yields to nothing but impossibilities," to heart. Once he set a goal for himself, he pursued it, regardless of any disappointments and discouragements.

PROFITING FROM THE CIVIL WAR

On April 6, 1862, the telegraph operator at the Detroit railroad depot posted incoming news about a great battle taking place in Shiloh, Tennessee.

Railroads and Telegraphy in the 1800s

Railroads and telegraphy were making rapid changes in American life throughout Edison's boyhood. The first railroad tracks in the United States were laid in the 1820s. By 1850, trains chugged throughout the eastern part of the country. During the Civil War (1861–1865), trains transported troops and supplies in both the North and South. By 1869, tracks stretched across the continent, quickly replacing wagon trains and boats.

As railroad tracks were laid down across the country, telegraph wires were strung right alongside them. The first telegraph line in the United States went up in 1843. By 1854, there were more than 23,000 miles (37,007 kilometers) of telegraph wire in operation. Not only did the telegraph operators send news through the wires, but they also sent information about trains, letting stations down the line know if they were on time, delayed, or stalled.

As Alva avidly read these reports, he thought of a way to sell far more than his daily one hundred newspapers.

He convinced his boss to sell him one thousand papers instead of his usual one hundred, and to sell them to him on credit. Then he convinced the Detroit telegraph operator to wire the headline, "60,000 Killed or Wounded at Battle of Shiloh" to each station on the way to Port Huron. As the train pulled into each station, crowds of people thronged to the train, wanting to buy newspapers so they could read the whole story. Alva sold all his papers. Not only had he made a huge profit, he learned first-hand just how powerful a tool both telegraphy and news stories could be.

This illustration shows a young telegrapher at work. The batteries on the shelf are connected by wires to the apparatus on the telegrapher's desk.

Tapping Telegrapher

After his lessons with MacKenzie, Alva obtained a job as an operator in Port Huron's tiny telegraph station, which was tucked into a corner of the town's jewelry shop. Telegraphy sets at that time were powered by batteries that produced electric current by submerging metal electrodes in a corrosive acid mixture. Part of Edison's job was to add more acid to the mixture when it was needed.

Experimenter that he was, he often added a bit more of one chemical or a bit less of another. According to one source, one day his mixture blew up, breaking glass and charring the shop. Edison had exploded himself right out of a job. But it was 1863, and the Civil War raged on. Telegraphers were in great demand. Edison packed his clothes, tools, electrical equipment, wire coils, and metal scraps and joined the hundreds of young telegraphers who traveled the country changing jobs almost as often as they changed their clothes.

FROM NOVICE TO FIRST CLASS

No one knows for sure when Edison started using his first name, but it was probably shortly after he left home. Over the next few years, he tapped out code in Michigan, Canada, Indiana, Ohio, Tennessee, and Kentucky. Along the way, he advanced from novice to first-class operator. Like most of his fellow telegraphers, he changed jobs often. Sometimes he quit a job to obtain a better position or salary. Sometimes he simply wanted to experience life in another part of the country. And sometimes he was fired for disrupting the office with his experiments.

Edison's real aim was to take press copy, stories transmitted by newspaper reporters in the field to their newspapers. To do that, he had to qualify as a first-class operator and take code at twenty-five to forty words a minute. He was not that fast, so he spent hours practicing, but then found a better way to take code. When telegraphy was first invented, operators used machines that recorded the dots and dashes of Morse code as pencil marks on a moving strip of paper. The operator read the code and then translated it into words. By the time Edison became a telegrapher, this step had been eliminated because operators were trained to transcribe words directly from the sounds of the dots and dashes.

Edison found a few old machines in a back room and connected them so that after the first machine recorded the incoming message, the strip of paper was fed into the second machine. Edison added a device that allowed him to control the speed at which it replayed the message. He practiced this way until his boss put a stop to it, but his practice machine had planted a firm idea in his head.

Telegraph messages could be sent only 200 miles (321.8 km) at a time. To send a message farther, it had to be relayed down the line by another operator. A message from Washington, D.C., required six separate relays to reach to Minneapolis, Minnesota. Edison knew that led to many errors. He thought if he could find a way to use the old machines to relay messages automatically, there would be fewer errors.

While working in an Indianapolis telegraph office in 1865, Edison made sketches and constructed models of a repeater telegraph. When he felt it was ready, he and a friend tested it, but it didn't work. Frustrated, Edison hurled the machine to the ground. Luckily, his friend picked it up. After Edison calmed down, he repaired the damage and continued tinkering. His boss yelled at him for wasting time on useless experiments when he should have been taking code, but Edison did not give up. He was convinced he could make his machine work. Although he was unable to

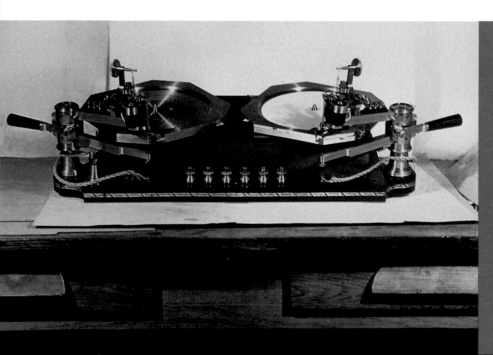

This is Edison's perfected repeater telegraph. The message was received on one side of the device and then automatically retransmitted through the second side.

perfect his repeater at that time, he knew the technology was important and continued to work on it.

Edison wasn't the only young telegrapher working on repeaters. Many other telegraph inventors were attempting to perfect one as well. Another advance in telegraph technology was the duplex telegraph, which could send two messages, each in a different direction, through the wires at the same time. Edison thought he could make a better duplex machine than anyone else. He lost one job when his boss yelled at him, "Any . . . fool ought to know that a wire can't be worked both ways at the same time." Edison persisted in his experiments. It took him many years, but eventually he did patent a duplex telegraph.

A TELEGRAPHER'S LIFE

Most young telegraphers spent their earnings and spare time on girls, drinking, and just having a good time. Edison didn't. He spent most of his money on supplies for his experiments, books on electricity and telegraphy, and novels. Most of his spare time was used for conducting experiments.

When he wasn't working or conducting experiments, he went to see plays with his friends, Milt Adams and Ezra Gilliland, whom he met while working in Cincinnati in 1865. Edison enjoyed the theater so much he considered becoming an actor, but his nervousness about speaking to an audience and his high-pitched voice soon changed his mind. Both Adams and Gilliland remained Edison's friends for many years and worked with him after he had set up his own businesses.

Most telegraph offices of the time were similar. Sixteen telegraphers and twelve clerks sat at large tables strewn with telegraph sets. Tangles of wires crisscrossed the room, leading from the sets to the main switchboard, then to the battery room in the back. The buildings were old and run down. They were hot in the summer, cold in the winter, and usually filthy. As they worked, the men joked, smoked cigars, and spat chewing tobacco at the ceiling.

Edison joined in the joking somewhat, but his deafness kept him from hearing much of their conversations. Although he couldn't hear the distracting noise, he was able to hear the code signals through the wires. He often said his deafness helped him to concentrate. He loved playing practical jokes on people, and used his creativity to invent devices to trick his fellow operators. One time, he took an old piece of electrical equipment he had found at a scrap yard and wired it to the office water bucket, so anyone who dipped his cup into it for a drink received an electric shock.

This illustration shows a telegraph office similar to the ones that Edison worked in.

Edison was the only one who found this funny. The men who got shocked were angry.

In the fall of 1867, Edison left his job in Cincinnati and returned to Port Huron for an extended visit. He found that his parents had moved out of their large home and into a much smaller one and that his mother was often depressed. That winter, Edison became ill and spent several months in bed. He was quite dejected. Then he received a letter from his friend Milt Adams, who was working for Western Union in Boston. Adams told Edison that if he came to Boston, he, too, could work for Western Union.

When Edison arrived in Boston in January of 1868, the city-bred operators there teased him about his country clothes—flannel shirt, shabby jacket, jeans several inches too short, and a hat with a torn rim. They had heard of his fondness for practical jokes and had one ready for him. Telling him they were testing his code speed, they had him take code from one of the fastest senders in New York. Edison scribbled, furiously trying to keep up. Then the sender started sending even faster by abbreviating many words. Edison sent back a message of his own: "Say, young man, change off and send with your other foot."

Edison got the job. He tapped the keys, played his water bucket trick on his fellow operators, and worked at his experiments. Boston was a hub of scientific innovation, especially in the fields of electricity and telegraphy. Edison met many other young telegraphers who were also hoping to become inventors. They often gathered at a large shop owned by Charles Williams, one of the city's leading inventors and sellers of telegraphic equipment.

One day, while browsing in a used bookshop, Edison found a great treasure—the three-volume set of Michael Faraday's books on electricity.

Michael Faraday, who had died only a few years earlier, was an English scientist who had been the first person to study the relationship between electricity and magnetism and had invented the first electric motor and dynamo. It was also Faraday's work with electromagnetism that made telegraphy possible. Edison now had two major role models: Thomas Paine and Michael Faraday.

Moving to the city of Boston offered Edison an opportunity to meet other inventors and to further explore his scientific interests.

"I am now twenty-one," Edison is reported to have said to his friend Milt. "I may live to be fifty. Can I get as much done as he [Faraday] did? I have got so much to do and life is so short, I am going to hustle."

PURSUING HIS DREAM

Edison worked the night shift at Western Union. He rented a corner in Williams' store, where he conducted experiments on his duplex telegraph during the day. Although Moses Farmer had demonstrated a duplex in 1856 and Joseph Stearns had demonstrated one in 1868, Edison felt his was better than either of theirs. Having learned the value of press coverage and self-promotion, Edison sent articles about his duplex to Franklin Pope, the editor of *The Telegrapher*, the leading journal of the industry and one of the country's leading telegraph inventors and experts. Pope like what he read, and he and Edison became friends.

Several months later, when Edison felt his duplex was ready, he borrowed money from a friend and took his device to New York to demonstrate it to Pope and his associate, James Ashley, who had succeeded Pope as editor of *The Telegrapher*. Both men were impressed with Edison's work.

Edison's goal at that point in his life was to quit his job and become a full-time inventor. To do this, he needed money—enough to live on and buy tools, equipment, and materials for his experiments. One way of raising the money was to borrow it, but he could never borrow enough. Another and better way was to attract investors. Investors do not give money away. They invest only to make a profit. In exchange for financial backing, Edison promised his investors the rights to use his patents to make and sell what he invented.

A VALUABLE LESSON FROM A FAILURE

Working as a press operator, Edison had often relayed stories to newspapers about bills passed by Congress. He knew it took many hours for a roll call to be taken to get a final tally. He invented a telegraphlike machine that could be set up by each representative's or senator's seat that recorded votes instantaneously.

He convinced one investor that this was a good idea and worked hard to perfect it. In November of 1869, he filed a patent application for his vote recorder. This was the first of more than a thousand patent applications he would submit during his long career.

Edison demonstrated his vote recorder to the legislatures in Washington, D.C., and in Massachusetts, but to his dismay, no one wanted one.

Edison's first patented invention was a telegraphic vote recorder.

Neither senators nor congressmen wanted to shorten the roll call method of voting. The longer the roll call took, the more time they had to give speeches to gather more support for their own bills.

The vote recorder was not the only device Edison was working on. He was also developing a telegraph that printed messages in words instead of in code, fire alarm systems, and even a facsimile telegraph that would transmit handwriting and pictures. Although he was not successful in patenting either the facsimile telegraph or the fire alarm system, he did patent his printing telegraph.

Surprised that his vote recorder did not sell, but not discouraged, Edison decided only to invent things he knew people wanted. He also decided it was time to pursue his dream full time. He placed a notice in *The Telegrapher*: "T. A. Edison has resigned his situation in the Western Union office, Boston, and will devote his full time to bringing out his inventions."

Rival Inventors

Edison was one of many young inventors working on telegraphic devices at this time. Some of the others were Edward Calahan, an employee of American Telegraph Company who invented the first telegraphic stock ticker, Franklin Pope, Alexander Graham Bell, Elisha Gray, and Nikola Tesla. Each time one of them made a new breakthrough and applied for a patent, the others were able to study that patent and apply the technology to their own work. So although they were competitors, they helped one another.

THREE

Fulfilling a Dream

Edison put his printing telegraph to use in a business he started with another young telegrapher, Frank Hanaford. They sent out stock quotes by stringing private telegraph lines to their clients' offices. Inventors often borrow ideas from one another, and Edison was no different. His stock-quoting printer was based on a design first invented by Edward Calahan, which was later improved by Franklin Pope. Pope's employer, Samuel Laws, offered a similar service in New York City. Private telegraph lines also provided a way for businesses to communicate with each other without using messengers to carry notes back and forth by hand.

Although Edison's and Hanaford's business serviced a number of accounts, Edison wanted to make further improvements to his printer. He also wanted to continue work on his duplex telegraph. But no one in Boston was willing to provide the funding he needed.

This advertisement announced Edison's business venture in partnership with Franklin Pope and James Ashley to the public.

ENTERING THE WORLD OF BIG BUSINESS

In January of 1869, Edison went to New York, hoping Pope could help him. Pope, who managed Samuel Laws's Gold & Stock Reporting Telegraph Company, offered Edison a cot in his workroom to sleep on, but said he couldn't help him in any other way. Discouraged, Edison wrote to his partner in Boston, "It is all I can do to keep the wolf from the door."

A few days later, the main machine at Laws's company stopped working. Within minutes, dozens of stock brokers' messengers stormed into the office, demanding the latest quotes. Edison examined the broken machine, saw what was wrong, and fixed it. He became the hero of the day and was hired to be Pope's assistant. Then Pope left the company and Edison took over as manager. For a few months, Edison was happy. He had a steady salary and the use of Laws's facilities to work on improving his printing telegraph. While he worked for Laws's, he made a number of improvements to the company's stock tickers and printers.

Within a few months, a competing company, Calahan's Gold & Stock Telegraph Company purchased Laws's company. They had their own manager, so Edison was once again without a job or resources. "The Consolidation . . . [and] my Consequent dismissal has upset all my calculations," he wrote to Hanaford.

A new opportunity opened for Edison when Pope and James Ashley invited him to join them in a new partnership. Edison was happy to do so. Pope, Edison & Company rented an office in Newark, New Jersey, and offered services as electrical engineers and contractors. Pope and Ashley provided funding while Edison worked on inventions, primarily his printing telegraph. The company also installed and maintained private telegraph lines, tested instruments for other inventors, helped other inventors file patents, and provided other services. A few months later, the trio started a second business, Financial and Commercial Telegraph Company. The company used a new printing telegraph that had been designed by both Edison and Pope, and with it they planned to compete with Gold & Stock. At that time, Ashley wrote in his journal that Edison was "a young man of the highest order of mechanical talent, combined with good scientific electrical knowledge and experience."

The second half of the 1800s was a period of intense commercial growth in the United States. Corporations and industries were expanding quickly and competition among them was fierce. This was particularly true in the telegraph industry. Each company wanted to beat the competition and control the industry by acquiring the patent rights to the many new devices Edison and other telegraphy inventors were designing. To do this, they bought out competing companies together with any patent rights the companies owned.

Marshall Lefferts, president of Gold & Stock Telegraph Company, wanted to eliminate competition from Financial and Commercial Telegraph Company. In February of 1870, he came to Edison with a deal. Without consulting with his partners, Edison agreed to design a facsimile telegraph and a new printing telegraph for Gold & Stock and to work as their consulting electrician for one year. The agreement also provided Edison with funds to set up a new lab and business in which he could work on these devices.

Edison then established Newark Telegraph Works, with a new partner, William Unger, an electrician recommended by Gold & Stock. Edison did not perfect his facsimile machine, but was successful in inventing and manufacturing other telegraphic devices. Later, Newark Telegraph changed its name to Edison and Unger. At the time he made the agreement with Lefferts, Edison was still in partnership with Pope and Ashley, but only until Gold & Stock bought Financial and Commercial Telegraph Company. After that buyout, Gold & Stock owned the rights to all of Edison's telegraphic inventions, including the ones he had invented together with Pope. Pope and Ashley were angry because Edison had made these agreements behind their backs. Ashley wrote in his journal that Edison was a "professor of duplicity and quadruplicity" who claimed others' inventions as his own.

Then another company, Automatic Telegraph, entered the picture. This company owned the patent rights to an automatic telegraph invented by an Englishman named George Little. An automatic telegraph worked differently from the more conventional one. Instead of an operator tapping code onto a keypad connected directly to telegraph wires, code was typed onto a keyboard that was attached to a stylus that punched the code onto a strip of chemically treated paper. The paper was then fed into a high-speed transmitter, which sent messages at speeds of one hundred words per minute or more. The problem was that Little's design was far from perfect and representatives from Automatic Telegraph Company asked Edison to design a better one. George Harrington, one of the principal investors of Automatic Telegraph Company, provided funds for Edison to set up another new company. They named it American Telegraph Company, and Edison opened a second shop in Newark in which to work on the automatic telegraph.

In October of 1870, Edison, who was only twenty-three years old, wrote to his parents, "I have one shop which Employs 18 men, and am Fitting up another which will Employ over 150 . . . I am now what 'you' Democrats call a 'Bloated Eastern Manufacturer.'" This was a bit of an exaggeration, but he did have two shops in which he and his employees carried on a variety of experimental and manufacturing projects, some for Gold & Stock, and others for Automatic Telegraph.

Edison put in long hours, often working late, and sometimes through the night, catching catnaps on a table or on the floor. He hired skilled technicians, mechanics, and machinists and with them built the core of what would become an expert and loyal staff, many of whom would follow him through many partnerships and business enterprises. Edison was an exacting but fair boss who expected his employees to work as hard as he did. Although he was younger than most of his employees, he called them his "boys," and they called him the "Old Man."

During this period, Edison worked mainly on developing the specific telegraphic apparatuses requested by his investors, but he worked on other experiments as well. Once when Harrington visited Edison's shop to check on the progress of the automatic telegraph, he complained that Edison was wasting time on useless experiments instead of concentrating on what he had ordered. Edison told him, "No experiments are useless." He explained that any experiment, successful or not, was valuable. Failed experiments, he said, taught him what would not work and often helped him figure out what would work. He also explained that many times, something he had learned in a failed experiment on one invention could later be applied to another invention.

In the spring of 1871, Edison signed yet another new agreement as contract inventor for Gold & Stock. At the same time, Western Union purchased Gold & Stock, so now Edison was working for both Automatic Telegraph and its main competitor, Western Union.

This became very complicated. Marshall Lefferts was the president of Gold & Stock, but he was also employed as the head of Western Union's stock reporting department, so he, too, was working for competing companies. He also had a financial interest in Automatic Telegraph. Not surprisingly, this led to many complications, both for Lefferts and for Edison.

LOVE AND MARRIAGE

While most of Edison's time and energy were taken up with his work, he had a life outside the shop as well. In 1871, when Edison was twenty-four years old, his mother died. He had been close to her and missed her deeply. Until that time, he had had few relationships with women. It is hard to separate the real facts from the many myths and stories that have accumulated about Edison and his life. Perhaps the loss of his mother made him think about marriage, or perhaps he decided that since he was now a successful businessman, it was time he married. At any rate, some months after his mother died, he met and fell in love with Mary Stilwell, a young woman who worked for one of the companies in which he was part owner.

Although Mary was only sixteen years old, the couple married on Christmas Day, 1871, after dating for three months. Marrying her boss was a step up the social ladder for Mary who came from a working-class family. No doubt she enjoyed the fine clothing and furnishings her husband provided for her, but marriage did little to change his work habits, and Mary soon found herself wishing he would spend more time at home with her and less time working. For his part, Edison wished Mary would take more of an interest in his work. A few months after their wedding, he wrote in his notebook, "My Wife Popsy Wopsy Can't Invent."

This photograph shows Mary Stilwell, at age sixteen, around the time she met Edison. According to a story printed in late 1800s, Edison proposed to Mary one day at work saying, "I've been thinking considerably of you of late, and if you are willing to have me, I'd like to marry you."

DEALS AND MORE DEALS

Marriage problems aside, Edison's main concerns remained business ones. By 1872, he had ended his relationship with American Telegraph Works. A short time later, he also ended his partnership with William Unger and formed a new one with Joseph T. Murray, a machinist with whom he had worked at American Telegraph Company. His dealings with competing companies continued. William Orton, president of Western Union, asked him to develop a better duplex than the one his company was using at the time. Although Edison had been working on a new duplex design for several years, he had never perfected it. He was happy to take up this work again, especially because Western Union would be providing the funding for it. Edison's work on this project led to his quadruplex telegraph, a device that could

Marion, Edison and Mary's daughter, immediately received the nickname "Dot" from her father.

send not two, but four messages simultaneously. Orton was interested in the quadruplex idea, but he refused to provide Edison with additional funding to work on it. George Prescott, one of Western Union's electricians, however, agreed to provide funding in return for half interest in any patents that came out of the experiments.

Edison began working in earnest on his quad. He was also working on several other things, while at the same time running his manufacturing business in Newark. Like most businessmen, he had accumulated several debts. Then, in 1873, a general economic panic occurred when a major bank failed and stock values plummeted. People who owed Edison money were unable to pay him, so he was unable to pay people to whom he owed money. He had to sell his house and move with Mary and their first child, Marion, who had been born on February 18, into a small apartment. He was in desperate need of ready cash. He asked Orton for money to continue his quad experiments. Orton made an offer, but Edison wanted more. They dickered back and forth for a few days. Then, before the deal was concluded, Orton left town for a business trip.

While Orton was gone, Jay Gould, a well-known financier and president of Atlantic & Pacific Telegraph Company, a rival of Western Union, told Edison he wanted to see the quad. He came to Edison's lab late at night and then asked Edison to accompany him back to his home, a large mansion in New York. He offered Edison $30,000 for the rights to use patents Edison might obtain for a multiple telegraph system. Gould's offer was larger than Orton's. Even though Edison had had a verbal agreement with Orton, he accepted Gould's deal. He also agreed to work as Atlantic & Pacific's electrician.

When Orton heard about Edison's deal with Gould, he was angry. He said Edison had made a commitment to Western Union. Several lawsuits followed. Western Union sued Edison and Gould. Edison sued Western Union. He also sued Gould because Gould never paid him what was promised. One lawsuit lasted for almost forty years.

By this time, Edison had many commitments to many different people. He was so busy fulfilling these obligations, he had no time to work on new experiments. Early in 1875, he ended his partnership with Murray, and with the cash he received from Gould, he paid off his debts and set up a new lab—this time without a partner. No longer would he commit himself to working for large corporations, nor would he get bogged down with manufacturing. Instead, he would concentrate only on experiments for new inventions. He also moved his family to a larger house and brought his widowed father and his nephew, Charley, to Newark to live with him.

He hired his nephew, along with John Kruesi and Charles Batchelor, two skilled employees with whom he had worked in his previous business. He also hired his old friend, Ezra

Charles Batchelor, one of Edison's most important assistants, was affectionately known as Batch. He worked with Edison throughout his career.

Gilliland, and a new employee, James Adams. He and Batchelor made lists of the many new ideas they would work on in the lab. One of these ideas turned out to be very successful. This was the electric pen, a copying device, powered by a small electric motor that used a stylus to push ink through holes in a stencil. This invention came about quickly. The first experiments on it began in the spring, and by the fall, Edison was marketing it.

Once again, Edison was involved in manufacturing. He placed Gilliland in charge of Edison's Autographic Press & Electric Pen and established a separate business to advertise and sell the pen. Despite the success of his pen and his desire to remain independent of large corporations, he found he needed more money to support his lab. When William Orton asked for his help, he once again contracted to work for Western Union.

Orton told Edison that two different men, Alexander Graham Bell and Elisha Gray, had shown him very similar new inventions based on a recent discovery, by another scientist, that music could be sent over wires. The new invention was an acoustic telegraph, which separated the tones of telegraphic signals and sent them as musical notes over telegraph wires. The advantage of this system was that multiple messages could be sent faster and farther. Orton asked Edison to come up with his own design for an acoustic telegraph. At the same time, he gave Edison a report describing a device made by a German inventor that sent actual speech over wires.

Edison began experimenting with acoustic telegraphy. He thought the papers on the transmission of speech were interesting, but did not plan to work on that project right away. While working on his acoustic telegraph, Edison and his assistants noticed that under certain conditions, bright sparks issued from the core of an electromagnet. Although these sparks carried no electrical charge, they seemed to penetrate materials that usually blocked electrical transmissions, such as glass and rubber. Edison thought the sparks were evidence of a natural phenomenon never before observed. He called this phenomenon "etheric force."

The Financial Panic of 1873

In the aftermath of the Civil War, there was a great deal of speculation in land, especially by railroad companies. Jay Cooke, one of the country's largest bankers, had lent a great deal of money to the Northern Pacific Railroad and had handled most of the government's wartime loans. In 1873, Cooke went broke when the railroad company and other debtors were unable to pay their loans. This set off a general financial panic. The stock market was closed for ten days. Banks could not extend credit. Many people lost their homes and businesses. Manufacturers, unable to meet their payrolls, closed their factories, causing thousands of workers to lose their jobs. Most major railroads went bankrupt, as did other major industries. The immediate cause of the panic may have been the failure of Jay Cooke's bank, but in truth, the causes had begun long before. People in the railroad industry and others purchased large tracts of land on which to build railroads. They invested large amounts of money in laying track and establishing new railroad lines. To do this, they went into debt, which they could not always pay back.

The economy remained depressed until 1878, but the memories of what had happened remained. Many people came to feel that industry owners were reaping huge profits, while the workers in those industries labored long, hard hours for little pay. This tension continued to grow and led to decades of labor unrest that eventually led to the formation of unions.

Edison conducted several experiments on etheric force, speculated on its possible practical applications, wrote articles, and even gave lectures about it. Most of the scientific community scoffed at his claims. Edison never gave up on an idea if he thought it was a good one, but he also had vowed only to invent practical devices. Because he saw no practical application for his etheric force, he put it aside. Perhaps he should not have done that, for many years later, this phenomenon turned out to be the foundation of radio and wireless communication.

A NEW DIRECTION

Once again Edison wanted to separate his manufacturing and inventing enterprises. He also wanted to get away from the noise and distractions of the city. Toward the end of 1875, he purchased several acres 12 miles (19.3 km) south of Newark and 25 miles (40.2 km) southwest of New York City in Menlo Park, New Jersey, a tiny hamlet of only six houses. There he planned to build a new laboratory in which he could concentrate on researching and developing new ideas.

Thomas Alva Edison, Jr. (right) was called "Dash" by his father. He is shown here with his brother William who was born a few years later.

FOUR

A New Kind of Workplace

During the winter of 1875, Edison and his top assistant, Charles Batchelor, drew plans for the new lab, and Edison hired his seventy-one-year-old father to supervise its construction. Never before had an inventor had a facility like the one Edison envisioned. It was a place large enough to experiment freely on whatever came to mind—not a workshop like his previous labs had been.

The lab was completed in March of 1876. Edison moved his family into a house that had come with the property. His family had grown considerably. In addition to Mary and three-year-old Marion, whom he had nicknamed "Dot," he now had a son, Thomas Alva, Junior, whom he nicknamed "Dash," who had been born in January. Sam Edison returned to

Ohio, but nephew Charley remained as part of Edison's family, as did Mary's sister and three domestic servants.

Charles Batchelor and John Kruesi, Edison's chief machinist, who also had families, purchased two of the six existing homes in the village, while unmarried employees found housing in the village boarding house. Edison and his lab had taken over Menlo Park.

THE MENLO PARK LAB

The two-story lab was around 100 feet (30.5 meters) long and 30 feet (9.1 m) wide. A picket fence barred wandering cows from drifting onto the long front porch and into the double doors that led to a reception area and Edison's office. Drafting tables, cabinets full of delicate telegraph instruments, and work tables that quickly became littered with wires, electrical devices, and other miscellany filled the main room of the first floor. Also, on the first floor were a carpentry room and machine shop. On the upper floor, a balcony looked out over farm fields. Inside was a large open room lined with shelves displaying bottles of chemicals, thousands of old machine parts, and work tables.

The first projects worked on at Menlo Park were experiments to perfect Edison's acoustic and multiple telegraphy systems. After the lab was set up, Batchelor commuted daily to New York, where he resumed his position as head of Edison's Autographic Press and Electric Pen business. Adams acted as Edison's chief assistant at the lab.

That summer, Edison's automatic telegraph system and his electric pen won prizes at the 1875 Centennial Exhibition in Philadelphia. But the star attraction of that show was a brand-new invention by Alexander Graham Bell.

WHO REALLY INVENTED THE TELEPHONE?

Edison knew that Bell had been working on acoustic telegraphy, just as he and another inventor, Elisha Gray, had been. While Edison concentrated on acoustic telegraphy, both Bell and Gray had turned their attention to a machine that could transmit actual human conversation instead of electrical beeps or musical tones—the telephone.

It is not unusual for several inventors to work on similar ideas at the same time, but it was unusual for two inventors to come up with ideas as similar as those of Bell and Gray and to complete them at the same time. On February 14, 1876, Bell submitted a patent application and Gray submitted a caveat—an official notice of intent to file a patent application—for a telephone. Patent disputes followed, but the Patent Office said Bell's patent application had arrived at the office before Gray's caveat, so Bell was awarded the patent. Although his telephone was far from perfected, Bell planned to start a company offering telephone service.

Western Union didn't want to be left out of this new aspect of the communications business, so William Orton asked Edison if he could make a better telephone. Basically, a telephone is a pretty simple device. It contains a diaphragm, or a thin, flexible disk, that vibrates when struck by sound waves, such as human speech. A mechanism converts the vibrations into electrical impulses, which are transmitted to a receiver, where they are converted back into sound.

Bell's telephone had two major flaws that Edison wanted to fix. First, the speaker had to shout into the instrument, and even then, the person on the other end could hardly hear what was said. Second, the telephone worked only for distances 2 miles (3.2 km) or less apart. Edison and his assistants began working on the telephone in June of 1876. First, they attacked the sound quality problem. As he did with so much of his work, Edison borrowed ideas from one invention to apply to another. In his experiments on automatic telegraphy, he had devised a carbon rheostat, a device that regulates the amount of electric current passing through a wire. He used this technology and added a diaphragm to it.

Along with their early work on improving the telephone transmitter, Edison and his crew continued their work on experiments on telegraphy technology, the etheric force, and other inventions. Edison also sometimes took on other projects as well. One of these was for a paper barrel company looking for a waterproof varnish, which resulted in a new waterproofing process that Edison patented. Nonetheless, his main focus remained the telephone.

In January of 1877, Edison scribbled in his notebook, "Succeeded in conveying over wires many articulated [clear] sentences. . . ." But the team still had a long way to go. Then, in February, they made a significant advance.

With Bell's telephone the caller held the receiver to his or her mouth to talk, then turned it around to listen. Edison decided to use two separate parts—one for listening and one for speaking. His transmitter not only produced better sound quality, but was also able to transmit over much longer distances. Edison applied for a patent for this innovation in April of 1877, but because of a long string of patent infringement lawsuits between him and Bell, it was fifteen years before he received it.

In spite of the long hours they worked, Edison and his team found moments to relax. They played music and sang songs together. Sometimes Edison, who loved to fish, dropped a fishing line into his stocked trout pond in back of the lab. He also enjoyed feeding a small black bear they had found wandering nearby, which they had kept chained to a post. One day, the bear broke loose and blundered into the lab, where it wreaked havoc.

Edison and his crew pose in front of a building in Menlo Park. In the top row (from left to right), there are Albert Herrick, Francis Jehl, Samuel Edison, George Crosby, George Carman, Charles Mott, John Lawson, George Hill, and Ludwig Boehm. In the middle row, there are Charles Batchelor, Edison, Charles Hughes, and William Carman. The two people in the bottom row are William Holtzer and James Hipple.

THE HARD WORK OF INVENTING

Edison and Batchelor had been trying to improve the sound quality of their telephone transmitter by adjusting the amount of pressure exerted against the diaphragm. Years earlier, Edison had designed a carbon rheostat in which he had used glass tubes filled with powdered graphite, a form of carbon. Those experiments were abandoned when he discovered that he could not obtain a steady rate of resistance because whenever the glass tubes were jostled, the resistance changed. Now, though, for the telephone receiver, he wanted variable resistance, so he began experimenting with carbon as one of the main components in his transmitter.

On July 17, 1877, Edison jotted in his notebook, "Telephone perfected this morning at 5 A.M. articulation perfect." Of course, the telephone was

This notebook entry shows Edison's early sketches for the telephone.

far from perfected at that point and Edison knew it, but he had complete confidence that with further experiments, it would be.

While working on these experiments, Edison said, "My mind was filled with theories of sound vibrations and their transmissions by diaphragms." He once wrote to a friend, ". . . I am so deaf that I am debarred from hearing all the finer articulations & have to depend on the judgment of others. . . ." In some of the experiments, Edison clamped a piece of metal between his teeth and held it against the receiver so he could feel the sound vibrations though his teeth.

At the same time Edison was working on diaphragms for his telephone transmitter, he was also conducting experiments on an improved version of an automatic-repeater telegraph, and, as was often the case, what he learned from working on one project helped him with another. While working on the telephone, he had noted that the diaphragm vibrated in response to the human voice. Earlier, he had used his teeth to help him feel the vibrations. Now, he attached a short needle to the diaphragm, held his finger against the needle, and spoke into the diaphragm so he could feel how hard the needle pressed against his finger to help him judge the variations in the loudness and softness of his voice. But the experiment also provided him with a new idea. He wrote in his notebook, "There is no doubt that I shall be able to store up and reproduce automatically at any time in the future the human voice perfectly." The idea of recording human speech intrigued him, but the job at hand was to perfect his telephone transmitter.

Edison and his assistants plowed on with experiments using carbon in the telephone transmitter. Lab notebooks from the fall and winter of 1877 show the results of more than two thousand experiments working with different carbon compounds. Eventually, the team devised a small button made of carbon that, when placed in front of the diaphragm, brought them closer to the result they wanted. The volume problem was then solved and that carbon button is still used in many telephones. Another surprise was that not only had Edison perfected the telephone, he invented the microphone at the same time.

Edison continued to refine his carbon-button transmitter and eventually sold his design to Western Union. Bell improved his own design by using a device based on a different carbon telephone transmitter designed by inventor Emile Berliner. Then, for several years, Bell Telephone and Western Union battled each other to control the industry, not only in the United States, but also in the United Kingdom, Europe, and Asia. Edison said, "Western Union [was] pirating the Bell receiver, and the Boston [Bell] company was pirating the Western Union [Edison's] transmitter." The success of Edison's carbon button transmitter for the telephone added to his growing international reputation as an inventor.

Batchelor and Charley Edison worked on the carbon button transmitter for a long, long time.

Edison's Assistants

Edison's talented assistants, many of whom remained with him throughout his career, were an integral part of nearly every one of his inventions. Edison was sometimes criticized for not including his assistants' names on his patents, but he did acknowledge their contributions by giving them a percentage of the profits earned on the devices they worked on, and later with stock in his companies. Many of them became quite wealthy.

This was especially true for Charles Batchelor, John Kruesi, James Adams, William Dickson, Francis Upton, John Ott, and Sigmund Bergmann. John Ott, who worked as one of Edison's machinists and draftsmen for nearly fifty years, once told an interviewer why he and others were willing to work so hard for him. "Because Edison made your work interesting," he said. "He made me feel that I was making something with him. I wasn't just a workman."

Among the many myths that have grown up around Edison are the stories of wonderful and unforeseen accidental discoveries that led magically into new inventions. "Discovery is not invention," he said, "and I dislike to see the two words confounded. A discovery is more or less in the nature of an accident." Edison said that a discovery is not something a person invents, but it is valuable and important. One such discovery occurred while he was working on the telephone, and it did lead to something quite remarkable.

The late 1870s were a hectic time for Edison.
He and his team were involved in a dizzying
number of projects.

FIVE

The Incredible Talking Machine

With several projects in various stages of completion, life at the Menlo Park lab was hectic. Edison said, "I start with the intention of going there," he once said, "but when I have arrived part way . . . I meet with a phenomenon, and it leads me off in another direction—to something totally unexpected."

For a good part of 1877, Edison was working first on improving the sound transmission for acoustic and automatic telegraphy, and later, on a better telephone transmitter. During those experiments, he had considered the possibility of not only transmitting voice sounds, but of the possibility of saving the messages to be replayed later.

PLAYING WITH SOUND

Most of Edison's inventions had to do with telegraphy and were primarily meant for business applications. He thought of the telephone as one more advancement in this technology. Messages sent by telegraph were recorded on paper, thus providing permanent records of business communications. He felt that if he could somehow create permanent records of telephone messages, the device would be more saleable. No one at that time foresaw that almost every home would contain a telephone meant for personal use.

Edison decided to apply some of the technology used in automatic telegraphy to accomplish this. In July of 1877, he attached a needle to a diaphragm. Next, he placed the needle against a cylinder covered with a roll of coated paper. Then, he pulled the paper toward him and at the same time shouted "haloo" into the diaphragm. As he expected, the needle made marks on the paper.

Edison recorded his work on the phonograph in his notebook.

Then he pulled the paper back to where the marks began. Once again he pulled the paper under the needle. The needle retraced the marks. He wrote in his notebook, "We heard a distinct sound, which with a strong imagination might have translated into the original 'Haloo.'"

Edison had come up with a brand-new invention, something that no one else had done—a machine that could record and play back the human voice. He named his new invention the phonograph, from the Greek words for sound and write. For the next few months, while he and his assistants continued their experiments on the telephone and telegraph, Edison filled his notebook with rough sketches of ideas for his new invention. Around this same time, he also fiddled with a few experiments on lighting, but quickly returned to the more immediate demands of perfecting the carbon button for his telephone transmitter.

As always, Edison was as busy with business arrangements as he was with his experiments. In September of 1877, he negotiated a deal to market his telephone design in Canada and completed the sale of his telephone transmitter to Western Union. He was also negotiating a deal to market his telephone and telegraph designs in Europe by selling patent rights to manufacturing companies there. Alexander Graham Bell, who had also set up telephone companies in Europe, sued Edison, claiming the telephone Edison wanted to market in Europe was infringing on his patents. That meant Edison had to come up with a new and different design that would not infringe on Bell's patents.

In September, Edison and his top assistants took a much-deserved break for a short fishing trip. When they returned, work in the lab continued on the telephone. All the while he was working on the telephone, Edison was thinking about his new invention.

IT SPEAKS

During the first week of December of 1877, Edison gave John Kruesi a drawing of how he thought his phonograph would work and asked him to construct a functioning model of it. "The machine must talk," he said. Kruesi agreed, but didn't think it would work. On December 6, the model was ready. It consisted of a rotating cylinder turned by a hand crank and a diaphragm connected to a needle on each end. All this was mounted on a brass base. The "boys" gathered around and bet the "Old Man" a box of cigars that his device would fail.

Edison paid no attention. He swept his hair off his forehead, bent over the machine, and carefully wrapped a sheet of tinfoil around the cylinder. That done, he leaned close to one of the diaphragms and shouted the nursery rhyme "Mary Had a Little Lamb" into it.

Edison shows off his first phonograph.

The room must have been quiet with anticipation as the crew members made ready to laugh at their boss's foolishness. Edison cranked the cylinder back to the beginning. He carefully placed the second diaphragm and needle in the groove that had already been made and then turned the crank again. To everyone's amazement, they heard a reproduction of Edison's voice reciting the rhyme. "I was never so taken aback in all my life," said Edison.

No one slept that night, nor did they work on any other experiments. Instead, they played with their new toy, talking into it and then listening to their own voices. Work on the phonograph proceeded rapidly. That night, Batchelor's notebook entry read, "Finished the phonograph. Made model for P.O.[Patent Office]."

The next day, December 7, Edison brought his new machine to the editor of *Scientific American* magazine in New York City. As Edison set the machine down and turned it on, the entire editorial staff crowded around the desk, waiting to see what would happen. When the machine spoke to them, they could hardly believe their ears.

The feature article of the next issue of the magazine was about the phonograph. "The machine began by politely inquiring as to our health, asked how *we* liked the phonograph, informed us that *it* was very well and bid us a cordial good night."

Edison filed his patent application for his phonograph on December 15, 1877. Always a businessman as well as an inventor, he immediately made plans to manufacture and market it. Over the next few months, he worked on improving his new invention. He also designed a number of talking toys and clocks.

Meanwhile, at the lab, work continued on further improvements to the carbon-button telephone receiver. Some time earlier, Edison had demonstrated his telephone to British electrical engineer William Preece, who worked for the British post office. Edison was hoping to sell his telephone design to them. The biggest stumbling block in this was coming up with a design that would not infringe on Bell's patents. Edison assigned this demanding task to his nephew, Charley Edison, who had been working at the lab for some time, and to Batchelor. James Adams had already taken some of these telephones to England, where he was testing them with the British post office.

THE WIZARD OF MENLO PARK

Edison received his patent for the phonograph less than two months after he applied for it. Most patent applications took a minimum of several months to process, and if there were any questions of duplication, they could take years, but the phonograph was so novel that no one else had applied for a patent on anything even remotely like it.

In April of 1878, the Edison Speaking Phonograph Company was established to sell his phonograph and his telephones in Australia and Central and South America.

Edison demonstrated his novel invention to fellow scientists and to the public. He even hired an agent to arrange phonograph performances in concert halls around the country. He called the phonograph his "baby," and said "I expect it to grow up and be a big feller and support me in my old age."

Edison and his machine were widely publicized in newspapers and magazines. Visitors flocked to Menlo Park by the hundreds to see the man one reporter called the "Wizard of Menlo Park." Edison loved the publicity and attention and happily escorted sightseers through the laboratory, showing off his extensive library and the piles of blueprints and mechanical designs that were scattered around work tables. Visitors also saw hundreds of bottles of chemicals, various kinds of metals, and batteries. They were awed by strange electrical machines like the one Edison called an "aerophone," which was a megaphone with huge "ears" that, it was claimed, could hear cows munching on grass 2 miles (3.2 km) away.

Dressed in his usual sloppy work clothes and speaking in his folksy Midwestern twang, Edison explained how everything worked and invited questions. After watching a demonstration of the phonograph, one man said, "I understand it all, except how the sound gets out again."

Long before he had begun working on the phonograph, Edison had been invited to exhibit his telephone and other inventions at the

This illustration depicts Edison as the "Wizard of Menlo Park."

Paris Universal Exposition in France. Naturally, he added the phonograph to his other exhibits.

PERFORMANCE FOR THE PRESIDENT

On April 18, 1878, Edison traveled to Washington, D.C., to demonstrate his phonograph to the National Academy of Sciences and to Congress. President Rutherford B. Hayes invited Edison to the White House for a personal demonstration, about which Edison said, "The exhibition continued till about 12:30 A.M., when Mrs. Hayes and several other ladies who had been induced to get up and dress, appeared. I left at 3:30 A.M."

Edison continued refining his invention, but something was troubling him. He had vowed to only invent things with a practical application. Edison predicted many possibilities for the phonograph: letter writing and dictation; books which would "speak" to blind people; teaching speech and elocution; preserving speeches of famous people; preserving family sayings; creating talking clocks, and making an educational tool for teachers. But most of these things had to wait until the phonograph underwent further refinements.

A Doll for His Daughter

During the summer of 1877, while working with diaphragms, Edison made a mechanical doll that sawed wood for his daughter. The doll had a funnel on top of its head that was connected to a mechanism that activated a little pulley inside the doll's body. When Marion spoke into the funnel, the little doll began sawing wood.

At the end of the summer of 1877, Edison decided that his "baby" had a long way to go before it would be of any commercial value and put it aside to work on other things. It was ten years before he worked on the phonograph again—only after other inventors had come out with their own designs. No way Edison was going to let another inventor get ahead of him.

MEASURING THE HEAT OF THE SUN

One of the other inventions Edison was working on during this period was his tasimeter, a device used to measure minute gradations of temperature. When he was invited to join a scientific expedition to Rawlings, Nevada, to view a rare solar eclipse and test his device, he gladly accepted. The eclipse was on July 29. His tasimeter did not work very well, and he never developed it further.

After the eclipse, Edison and a group of other scientists traveled through the West camping out and sleeping under the stars. Edison explored a silver mine to see if it might be feasible for him to develop a special machine to extract ore more efficiently than using a pick and axe. This was another idea he would go back to later. While on his trip, he was elated to hear that he had won the grand prize for his inventions at the Paris Universal Exposition. But perhaps the most significant aspect of this trip was the long discussions he and the other scientists held around their campfires, speculating about the possibility of using electricity as a source of power to provide lighting and heat. He returned to Menlo Park refreshed and ready to begin work on what would become the largest and most daring project he would ever undertake.

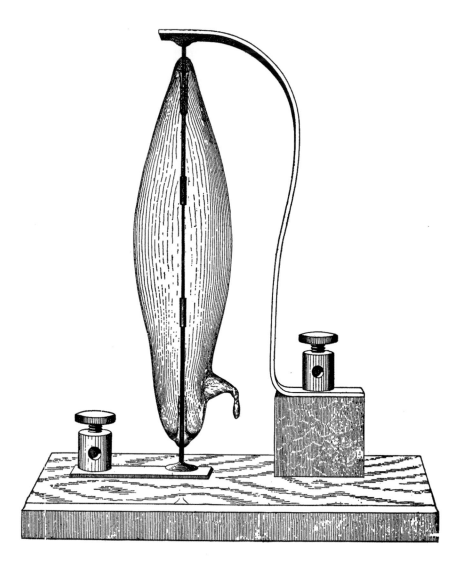

This illustration shows an early lightbulb developed by Joseph Swan, a British inventor and chemist. Swan had been experimenting with a form of incandescent lighting as early as 1848, only one year after Edison was born. Swan continued with his experiments, and eventually became one of Edison's major competitors for electric lighting in England. Eventually their differences were settled when their two companies merged.

Capturing Daylight

By 1878, scientists had been working on electric lighting for fifty years. Arc lighting, which worked by sending a strong electric current between two carbon rods, was already being used for streetlights and lighthouses, but was not practical for indoor lighting because it emitted poisonous gases and the light was too glaringly bright. Another type of light scientists had been experimenting with was incandescent light. This is the kind of light Edison wanted to make.

Incandescent means glowing, and the main feature of this type of light is a curved filament attached on either end to tiny electrodes and encased in a glass bulb. Moses Farmer and others had already produced primitive incandescent lights, but no one had yet figured out how to make the filament hot enough to give off light for more than a few minutes without it burning up.

Edison felt he could solve that problem. But electric lighting was only one part of his vision. He wanted to provide electric power to operate stoves, heating units, sewing machines, factory machines, elevators, and lots more. He also wanted to provide that power from a central power station. He felt that electric power would be more efficient, safer, and less expensive than the central gas lighting then in general use. His idea was to deliver the electricity in much the same way as gas companies delivered gas—through underground conduits, or tubes.

A GRAND PLAN

Because nothing like this existed, Edison first had to conceive of and then invent every component he would need. But first he had to achieve two things: perfect the incandescent light and figure out how to produce enough electricity to power a central system.

At that time, most electricity was produced by generators. In September of 1878, soon after he returned from his trip to Nevada, Edison and Batchelor traveled to Ansonia, Connecticut, to examine a new dynamo William Wallace had invented to power the arc lighting system he had installed at his factory. Edison liked what he saw and asked Wallace to build a dynamo for him.

When he returned to Menlo Park, he boasted to news reporters that he was perfecting an incandescent light and a system of electric lighting that would be far superior to gas lighting. He said he would build a central power system to light 1 square mile (2.6 square kilometers) in New York City, and that his perfected incandescent light would be ready in six weeks. The area he would light would include Wall Street, the center of the financial district. Also in that area were factories, apartment houses, and the offices of most of the city's newspapers.

When a reporter remarked that if he could really replace gas lighting, he would make a fortune, Edison said, "I don't care so much about making my fortune as I do for getting ahead of the other fellows." That was probably true, but only partly. Edison had already made a lot of money from his other inventions and wanted to make lots more. He was also very competitive and wanted to be known as the world's leading inventor.

Some people were sure Edison would fulfill his promise. After all, he was the wizard who had produced the phonograph. Others were sure he would fail. Edison needed a great deal of financial backing for this project, and his knew his boasting would incite the interest of new investors. Edison relied on his attorney, Grosvenor Lowry, to handle negotiations with a number of powerful financiers and bankers who joined with Western Union to form Edison Electric Light Company. This company was established on October 16, 1878. If his system did all Edison promised, he could expect to earn a royalty of $30,000 a year. At a time when an average working man's salary was less than $1,000 a year, that was a great deal of money.

Meanwhile, Edison had already executed the first of what would be many patent applications for his light, and he and his crew were busily conducting experiments. Edison knew from his own and others' earlier experiments that he needed a thin, spiral-shaped filament made of a material that would get hot enough to give off light, yet not burn up. He also knew he had to enclose this filament in a vacuum—inside a glass tube from which as much air, or oxygen, as possible had been pumped out. He also knew that with current technology, there was no way to achieve a complete vacuum, so he planned to add a mechanical regulator to his bulb that would help to control the heat.

Edison knew other inventors had tried both carbon and platinum as filaments. Both materials are good conductors of electricity, but carbon oxidizes, or burns up, quickly, so he chose to work with platinum, a rare and very expensive metal that has a high melting point and is slow to oxidize. Experiment after experiment at the lab produced nothing but frustration. No filament burned for more than a few minutes. Edison knew his boastful estimates of early success were exaggerated, but hadn't realized just how exaggerated they were.

DELAYS AND SETBACKS

The lightbulb was only one part of Edison's vision, so while work continued on that, he and his assistants were also working on generators that would power the electrical system as well as the other components the system would need. Edison decided that Wallace's generator was not powerful enough, so he ordered others. He and Batchelor studied these and he began designs for a new and better generator than any that already existed.

After working furiously for a few weeks, Edison, exhausted and frustrated, fell ill and was forced to spend a few days in bed. That same week, on October 26, 1878, Mary delivered their third child, a son named William Leslie. Mary was in a weakened condition from a difficult pregnancy and required a good deal of special care. Edison, though, recovered from his illness and returned to work to face other problems.

The patent applications he filed for his intended lightbulb were contested by other inventors who claimed they had already invented one.

Under pressure from his investors who did not want to get bogged down in lawsuits, he hired Francis Upton to conduct a thorough study of all prior patents and inventions having to do with lighting. Upton, who had degrees in science and math, was the first person Edison hired who had university training. He stayed on with Edison to become his chief scientific assistant and mathematician.

With some of the money he received from his investors, Edison also hired other new employees, added a new machine shop in which to build and test generators, and built an elaborate new library and office suite at his Menlo Park facility. In the lab, month followed month as different filament materials and glass bulbs were tested.

By November of 1878, the investors were becoming concerned about the vast amounts of money Edison was spending and wanted to see some results. After all, he had predicted an early success. On the advice of his lawyer, Edison agreed to provide a demonstration of the experiments, even though none of them had yet been completely successful. To offset the investors' fears, he told them, "The first step is an intuition and comes in a burst," he said. "Then difficulties arise. This thing gives out and then that. 'Bugs,' such as little faults and difficulties are called, show themselves. Months of intense study and labor are required before commercial success—or failure. . . . I mean to succeed."

If his system were to be successful, his lightbulb had to be cheap, both to produce and to use so that the average consumer could afford to buy and use them. Platinum was expensive because it was rare, so he began an intensive search for a plentiful, and thus, less inexpensive supply of it. He sent letters to hundreds of mining companies all over the world, but when it became apparent that there was no cheap source of this metal, he began experimenting with platinum alloys and other metals. At one point, he even tried using piano wire.

In the spring of 1879, after several preliminary designs and experiments, Edison had invented a powerful new generator that was nicknamed "Long-Legged Mary." The generator was so powerful that a whole new idea occurred to Edison. He knew that small amounts of platinum were often found in certain kinds of sand and rock. Perhaps his new generator could be used to run special machinery to pull minute quantities of the rare metal from those materials. So along with working on creating his electric system, he started working with mining experiments. Although his idea of extracting platinum from sand did not work, his foray into mining experiments would continue. A few months later, in December of 1879, he organized the Edison Ore Milling Company.

Meanwhile, experiments on the lightbulb continued. Edison's team had yet to produce a bulb that did not break when it was heated, nor had they found a way to produce a complete vacuum within the bulb. This problem was overcome after he hired Ludwig Boehm, a German glassblower, in August. He ordered several different types of vacuum pumps, and with Boehm's help, designed a new and better one—just as he had with the generator.

CARBON HERE, CARBON THERE

While Edison and his helpers were working on the lightbulb and lighting system, experiments continued on other projects, particularly the carbon-button telephone receiver they were designing for use in England. In February, Edison sent his nephew Charley to England to demonstrate the system to British officials, and in May, the British Parliament approved the formation of the Edison Telephone Company of London. Edison was elated. He used the $5,000 he received as an advance payment to purchase new books for his library and also made his wife happy by presenting her with $1,000.

Although the sale was made, there were still many bugs to work out with the carbon button, and work on it continued throughout the summer and into the fall of 1879. It was during this work that Edison experienced one of those lucky sparks of inspiration. The carbon buttons were made from lampblack, which was scraped from the glass chimneys of kerosene lamps kept burning day and night for this purpose.

One night during the first week of October of 1879, Edison was sitting in the lab absentmindedly rolling some of this lampblack between his fingers. When he looked at what he had done, he saw a slender tube of carbon. He knew he needed a slender spiral for his lamp filament. He also knew carbon possessed certain qualities he needed for his filament, but that it burned up too quickly. He thought about the new vacuum pump and stronger bulbs he and Ludwig Boehm had developed. Maybe, he thought, with these improvements, a carbon filament would work.

Edison and Batchelor conducted two weeks of intensive experiments, trying to make a filament from the lampblack. The experiments told them they were on the right track, but that pure lampblack was not what they needed. In the course of their experiments, Edison decided that whatever they carbonized must be a naturally fibrous vegetable material. Cotton sewing thread fit the bill. It was the right thickness and was a natural fiber. Time after time, they folded lengths of thread into a hairpin shape and carbonized them in a kiln. But each time the carbonized thread crumbled when they tried to lift it out of the mold.

SAD NEWS AND SUCCESS

On October 17, Edison received a cable from Europe informing him that Charley Edison was gravely ill. A few days later, another cable arrived saying that Charley had died. Everyone at the lab was upset, but they carried on with their experiments. Because Charley had done so much work selling the carbon button, he had made an important contribution to the latest lighting experiments.

On October 22, 1879, Batchelor reported the group's first big breakthrough with a carbon filament. His notebook indicates that this was the ninth test in their latest set of experiments. "We made some very interesting

Edison and his Family

Though Edison left his family at young age, he remained close with them throughout their lives. He took a special interest in his brother William's son, Charles Pitt Edison, and sent him science books and special science lessons were prepared for him by Charles Batchelor. When young Charley was twelve years old, he made the first of many visits to his uncle's home in New Jersey, and by the time he was fifteen, young Charley was already working in his uncle's lab.

When Edison purchased land in Menlo Park, he sent for his father, Samuel, who supervised the building of it. Both Samuel and Charley lived with the Edisons in their Menlo Park home. Charley became a full-time member of his uncle's staff, helping with experiments and acting as Edison's photographer and personal assistant. Later, Charley became an important member of the team working on the carbon button telephone.

experiments on straight carbon made from cotton thread," he wrote. He noted that they had taken a very thin strand of sewing thread and carbonized it by placing it in a small, enclosed chamber and baking it in an oven. When the filament was ready, they inserted it into a bulb from which all the air was evacuated. This lightbulb remained lit for more than thirteen hours—the longest time they had yet achieved. "If it can burn that number of hours," Edison said, "I know I can make it burn a hundred."

In their search for a better filament, Edison and his assistants carbonized a variety of different materials, each noted in Batchelor's notebook: vulcanized fiber, celluloid, boxwood shavings, coconut hair and shell, various types of drawing paper, shavings from several types of wood,

Edison and his crew test one of the many carbonized materials in their efforts to find the perfect filament for their lamp.

tissue paper string, cotton lampwick, cork, and other materials. Throughout that summer and fall, Edison and his assistants worked, often for days at a time. In spite of countless disappointments, Edison remained confident. When his staff became discouraged he bolstered their spirits by praising their efforts, setting up small competitions between them, and offering prizes and extra bonuses as incentives.

In early November, Francis Upton wrote to his family, "The Electric Light seems to be a continual trouble for as yet we cannot make what we want and see the untold millions roll upon Menlo Park that my hopes want to see. . . ." The investors, as well as the general public, wanted to know if any progress was being made. One reporter wrote, "As day after day, week after week, and month after month passes and Mr. Edison does not illuminate Menlo Park as he has so often promised to do, doubts as to the practicality and value of his widely advertised and much-lauded invention begin to be entertained in the public mind."

Then, on November 16, 1878, Batchelor wrote in his notebook that they had made the "first lamp that answers the purpose we have wished." He noted that this new filament was inexpensive as it was made from a piece of charred cardboard bent into a horseshoe shape and sealed in a glass bulb from which the air had been evacuated. Then a current of electricity heated the carbon to a brilliant whiteness "so that it will give a light equal to that from a good size gas burner."

It had been a little more than a year since Edison's first big announcement—far longer than he had promised, but not so very long considering the enormity of what he had done. He was finally ready to show the world what he had accomplished. He placed announcements in the newspapers that a public demonstration would be held on December 31.

NEW YEAR'S EVE SPECTACULAR

The lab, Menlo Park's tiny railroad station, and the village's six houses were wired for electric lighting. Although people had been coming to see what was going on since the announcement, more than three thousand visitors poured into Menlo Park on New Year's Eve. They had come to see what the wizard had conjured this time. As they streamed from the special excursion cars set up by the railroad, softly glowing lights atop wooden poles lit their way to the lab.

Edison, dressed in wrinkled work clothes, a half-buttoned vest, and a white handkerchief at his neck, greeted them and led them through the lab. Peering at a lit bulb, one man asked him how he got "that red hot hairpin" into the "bottle."

Edison repeated his early boasts, promising he would light up a square mile around Menlo Park, then neighboring towns, then Newark, and finally, New York City. He promised his bulbs would cost only 25 cents each and the electricity to light them would cost just pennies a day. The evening was a

This is a reproduction of Edison's first incandescent lightbulb.

huge triumph. After the crowds left, Edison and his crew celebrated around the pipe organ someone had given Edison as a gift. Edison even made up a special song for the occasion:

I am the wizard of the electric light

And a wide-awake wizard, too,

Quadruplex, telegraph, or funny phonograph

It's all the same to me.

With ideas I evolve and problems that I solve

I'm never, never stumped, you see.

The cardboard filament was a triumph, but only the first step along a very long road.

Lightbulbs—Then and Now

Edison's final bulb, which he invented in July of 1880, used a bamboo filament. It was encased in a clear glass bulb. Today's filaments are made from tungsten, a metal that can be spun very thin, has a very high melting point, and emits a very white light. Today's bulbs are filled with krypton gas that works even better than a vacuum to keep the filament from burning out.

SEVEN

Lighting the World

After his dazzling New Year's Eve display, Edison closed the lab to visitors so he and his crew could concentrate on the next phase of the project. They needed to invent and design the hundreds of components and small details that would make up the entire electrical power system. His boast that he would perfect the incandescent bulb in six weeks was far off—it actually took him fifteen months. It would take three more years for Edison to complete the entire system.

Edison's overall plan involved seven separate parts. The first two were well underway—creating an efficient lightbulb and powerful generators. He still needed to design a reliable wiring system to carry electricity from a central source to each user and devices to regulate the voltage. Then he needed to design a system of underground pipes to carry the wires from the central power station to each customer. He also needed fuses and

Edison stands in front of his first giant dynamo.

insulating materials to guard against short circuits and fires. In addition to all this, he needed to create sockets, lamps, and switches. And to make it all commercially useful, meters to measure how much electricity a customer used needed to be designed.

Edison's goal was not only to create a new lighting system, but to create one that would be less expensive than gas lighting. He conducted a door-to-door survey to find out how much gas was being used in the area for lighting and how much power would be needed to run elevators and other machinery so he could calculate costs.

Because there were so many different aspects of this giant project, his assistants took on even more important roles than they had previously held, often assuming almost full responsibility for what they were working on.

Edison spent most of his time at the lab putting in all-night sessions. Despite the sixty to eighty hours a week he and his employees worked, they were happy. Just as in his earlier businesses, he knew how to keep his employees' spirits high by praising them and by participating with them in contests to see who could produce the highest voltage from a hand-cranked generator or betting on how long each test lamp would remain lit before burning up. He and his crew often ate late dinners sent to the lab by one of the wives, and then sat around the lab pipe organ singing silly songs.

Even when he wasn't working, he seemed to enjoy the companionship of his assistants more than that of his family. Edison was happy at Menlo Park, but Mary was not. She missed the social life city living offered and felt that Edison neglected her and the children. She was often ill, suffering from what doctors called a nervous condition.

A MISSED OPPORTUNITY

Edison was concerned about his wife's health, but his work remained his top priority. In February of 1880, while working on the lightbulb, one of Edison's assistants noted a strange, blue glow inside the glass. When this occurred, the inside of the glass turned black. Edison figured this was caused by electric current passing through the filament. He inserted a small platinum plate into the bulb and tried to measure the current, but found none. He was amazed. Could electricity flow from the filament to the metal with no wire connecting them? He conducted experiments to find out what was happening, made careful notes of his observations, and decided this discovery might be useful as a voltage indicator and regulator. He filed a patent application for such a device, but never really did anything with it.

Just as he could not predict the importance of the etheric force he had discovered earlier, he did not know that his new discovery would become the basic principle of electronic transmission. Years later, it was this principal that led to the invention of vacuum tubes for radio and to the vast array of electronic instruments used today, such as television, radar, and wireless communications. William Preece, the British electrical engineer with whom Edison had worked on his telephone, later named this phenomenon the "Edison Effect."

PERFECTING THE BULB

Although they had a filament that worked fairly well, Edison and Batchelor were still seeking a better natural fiber than carbonized cardboard for the filament in the bulb. Edison spent months examining slices of bark, bits of rag, carpet fibers, wild grasses, segments of animal hides and hooves, strips of cornstalks, and much more under his microscope. He studied botany and sent scouts to pharmaceutical suppliers and even museums to search out every possible vegetable material. "Before I got through I tested no fewer than 6,000 vegetable growths, and ransacked the world. . . ," he said.

Then, one warm day in July of 1880, Edison picked up the bamboo fan he used to cool himself and took a close look at it. He cut a small strip off the rim and slid it under his microscope. Pleased, he cut more strips and asked Batchelor to carbonize them and test them as filaments. They worked! At last, they had found the perfect material, but they did not know where they could obtain a constant supply of bamboo. Certainly not in New Jersey.

Edison sent teams to Asia, India, and Central and South America to search for a reliable source. They chose one from Japan. Bamboo remained the filament in most lightbulbs for the next ten years. Then, most bulb makers switched to a humanmade cellulose compound. It wasn't until 1912 that the metal tungsten that is used today was adopted.

ANOTHER DIVERSION

Work progressed on Edison's electrical system, but slowly. However, things were never dull at Menlo Park. If something spectacular wasn't going on, Edison made something spectacular happen. From the time he was a small boy, he had been captivated by railroads. Railroads ran on steam power, but Edison wondered if an electric motor run by a large generator could be used instead.

In the spring of 1880, he had a crew lay a circle of track that wound its way up and down a small hill in a field opposite the lab. Edison designed and John Kruesi built an engine made from a large generator and attached it to a flatbed truck with metal wheels. Wires embedded in the track carried the electricity from the lab through the wheels to the engine. A transmission made of pulleys and gears provided power to the driving axle. Edison had built the very first electric train in the United States.

On May 13, crowds gathered alongside the track. Batchelor and Edison climbed on. The engine pulled an open car loaded with twenty riders. As Edison rang a bell to shoo cows out of the way, Batchelor drove the little train at 20 miles (32 km) per hour. Then, coming around a curve, the engine jumped the track, and the passengers had to push the little train back to its starting place.

A newspaper reported, "Mr. Edison has been relieving his labors by the erection of an electric railway." Several railroad people were interested

For fun, Edison built a railroad track and ran trains in Menlo Park.

and investors offered to back the forming of an Edison Electric Railway Co. Edison made improvements in his engine design and obtained patents, but said, "I could not go on with it [railroads]. I had too many other things to attend to, especially in connection with electric lighting." He did exhibit his engine at the Railway Exposition in Chicago in 1883, and soon after that, other people took up the idea. Years later, though, he did work on improving electric streetcars.

BIRTH OF A NEW INDUSTRY

Work progressed on the lighting system and by the fall of 1881, Edison was ready to begin constructing his central power station in New York. To do this, he moved his entire operation to the city. He bought a mansion on New York's fashionable Fifth Avenue for his office. There he installed a small version of his lighting system. When millionaires J. P. Morgan and Cornelius Vanderbilt saw what he had done, they ordered

Morgan and Vanderbilt: Financial Giants

When Edison sought investors to back his electric power project, he found himself associating with some of the country's leading industrialists and financial leaders, including John Pierpont Morgan and Cornelius Vanderbilt. The son of a banker, Morgan started out as a stockbroker and later ran his own brokerage and banking company. His empire grew to include railroad, steel, and other businesses. Vanderbilt began his career at the age of sixteen with a ferry service from Staten Island to Manhattan. He expanded his business over the years and controlled most of the trade on the Hudson River. He expanded his shipping business to build one of the first cross-country transportation lines, combining ships and trains.

Edison (left) stands outside the offices of Edison Electric Light Company at 65 Fifth Avenue in New York with Charles Batchelor and Major S. B. Eaton. Eaton was the president of this company.

private systems for their mansions. Edison soon had a side business installing private lighting systems.

At the start of this project, Edison's investors had formed the Edison Electric Light Company so Edison could develop the lightbulb, generators, and the other components of his system. Now that he was ready to begin work on the power plant, new companies were born. In December of 1880, investors provided money to establish the Edison Electric Illuminating Company of New York, which would first build and then run the central power plant. Factories would also be needed to manufacture the bulbs, light fixtures, sockets, fuses, fuse blocks, meters, voltage regulators, dynamos, and various other components. Edison wanted to control these ventures himself and hoped his investors would provide funding for these factories. The investors, however, didn't want to fund several different manufacturing ventures. They wanted the illuminating company to own all patents and then sell the rights to various manufacturers. Because the investors refused to help him build the factories, Edison said, "I will build the factories myself."

Edison established Edison Electric Lamp, Edison Machine Works, and other companies. He also set up a new laboratory in New York so he could continue his experiments, both on the electric lighting system and on other projects. Funding for these new companies was provided mostly by Edison himself, but several of his closest assistants also invested in them. Edison made those men the managers of the new companies. He assigned his patent rights to the companies in exchange for stocks and royalties. The assistants also received a percentage of the patent rights and considerable amounts of stock. Once again, Edison had proven himself as successful an entrepreneur as he was an inventor. With the establishment of all his new companies, he had started an entire new industry—the manufacturing and selling of electrical equipment.

Because he was working full time in New York, he brought his family to the city. They lived in a hotel across the street from his office. Mary, who had never been happy in rural Menlo Park, was delighted at first, and enjoyed giving fancy tea parties for fashionable ladies, but her happiness evaporated quickly. She had hoped Edison would spend more time at home with her, but he was busy working and she was just as lonely as she had been in Menlo Park.

THE POWER PLANT

Once his office was set up, Edison began work on the central power station located in an old building he purchased on Pearl Street in the center of the city's financial district and close to a number of small factories, shops, and apartment buildings. The first and largest part of the task was to rip up the street and lay underground conduits, which would carry the wires and conductors. John Kruesi headed up this job. He also oversaw the manufacture of the conductors and related components at one of the factories.

Shortly after this work began, in January of 1882, Mary became ill again, and Edison took time off to take her and the children to Florida. When they returned, they took up residence at the Menlo Park house and, for a few months, Edison worked at the lab there. That was the last time Edison lived at Menlo Park or worked at that lab. That summer, he spent most of his time in his New York lab or working at Pearl Street. Then, in the fall, he rented a large apartment in fashionable Gramercy Park and once again brought his family to the city.

Meanwhile, in July of 1881, he sent Batchelor to Europe to prepare exhibits of the lighting system at the Paris Electrical Exposition in France and at the Crystal Palace Exposition in London, England. Both exhibits garnered prizes, along with new fame and business opportunities for Edison. A London paper wrote, "Mr. Edison's exhibition is the wonder of the show."

That summer, Edison's typical day was a busy one. He woke early to catch a morning train to Menlo Park to check on a problem at the lamp factory there, then returned to New York to work at his office, the lab, or check on things at one of his other factories. He often worked alongside the men digging trenches and installing pipes. And he spent many nights supervising construction of yet another new generator.

Finally, in July of 1882, after a year of work and delays, the Pearl Street station was completed. It was time for a test run. "Of all the circuses since Adam was born," said Edison, "we had the worst then! One engine would stop and the other would run up to a 1000 revolutions. . . . It was a terrifying experience. . . . The engines and dynamos made a horrible racket . . . the place seemed to be filled with sparks and flames of all colors . . ." He admitted he had run the test too soon, but had been under great pressure. "I kept promising," he said. However, failure was never failure to Edison. He went back to work and fixed the problems. A few months later, the generators were fired up again. This time, everything worked.

The Electrical Age was launched at 3:00 P.M. on September 4, 1882, when an engineer threw the main switch at the Pearl Street station. Power flowed through more than 100,000 feet (30,480 m) of conduit to Edison Electric Illuminating Company's first eighty-five customers, providing power to four hundred lights. "I have accomplished all I promised," Edison said.

THE MENLO PARK YEARS

By 1883, most lab work was conducted in New York City, and the lamp factory had been moved to East Newark, New Jersey. Menlo Park had been in operation for only five years, but what years they were. It was there that Edison made the latest advances in telegraphy. It was there that he invented his phonograph and his carbon-button telephone. And it was there that he perfected the incandescent lightbulb and designed his lighting system.

Headlines of the Times

In 1881, while Edison was building the power station at Pearl Street, Barnum & Bailey's Greatest Show on Earth opened at Madison Square Garden, Czar Alexander II of Russia was assassinated, Clara Barton formed the first American chapter of the Red Cross, and the first American trade unions were organized.

More important than any single invention, though, was the precedent that Menlo Park set. With the development of the lighting system, Edison had demonstrated that the process of research and its resulting inventions was in itself an industrial process well worth investing in. Later, other industrialists borrowed the idea, and today, almost every industry has a research and development program.

EIGHT

New Directions

After the Pearl Street station was opened in 1882, Edison checked on his many factories, made sure Pearl Street was functioning properly, worked in his lab, and sometimes even took Sundays off. He also traveled around the country, establishing lighting systems in other cities and towns. In the winter, he took his family to Florida for a few months.

LIFE CHANGES

In the summer of 1884, Mary became gravely ill with what doctors called brain fever. It was probably a tumor. She died on August 9. Years later, Edison's daughter Marion recalled that the next morning, she found her father "shaking with grief, weeping and sobbing so he could hardly tell me that mother had died in the night."

After his wife's death, Edison seldom returned to Menlo Park. He became very close to Marion, who lived at a boarding school near his office. Edison had less of a relationship with his sons who continued to live at the Menlo Park house with Mary's sister, Alice, and her husband, who turned the old lab buildings into a chicken hatchery.

At thirty-eight years old, the once penniless young man who had quit his job in hopes of becoming an independent inventor was earning healthy royalties from his many patents and was one of the wealthiest inventors in the country. For the first time in his life, he spent time with friends and enjoyed a social life.

Mina relaxes with a group of friends at a summer picnic. She is the fourth person on the left.

During the winter of 1885, he met eighteen-year-old Mina Miller, who was accompanying her father at the World Industrial and Cotton Centennial Exposition in New Orleans. Edison was smitten with her youth and her "great dazzling eyes." A few weeks later, while in Boston visiting his friend Ezra Gilliland with whom he was working on a new set of experiments for Bell Telephone Company, Edison again met Mina, who attended school in Boston and was a friend of the Gillilands.

MINA ON HIS MIND

Later that summer, Edison visited the Gillilands again, but this time Mina was with her parents at their summer home in Chautauqua, New York. During his stay, Edison kept a personal diary in which he wrote, "Saw a lady who looked like Mina . . . came near to being run over by a streetcar. If Mina interferes much more will have to take out an accident policy."

This diary, kept for only two weeks, also contains several rambling entries that reveal a side of Edison very different from the no-nonsense self he portrayed in the business world. In one entry, he wrote, ". . . This is by far the nicest day of this season, neither too hot nor too cold—it blooms on the apex of perfection—an Edenday. Good day for an angels' picnic. They could lunch on the small flowers and new mown hay, drink the moisture of the air, and dance to the hum of bees . . ." The diary gives an insight into the way his mind darted quickly from one subject to something seemingly unrelated. Perhaps it was this ability that helped him conceive many of his innovative ideas.

Later that summer, he joined the Gillilands when they went to Chautauqua to visit Mina's parents. Not only was Edison smitten with Mina, but he found much in common with her father who, like Edison, was an

This portrait was taken of Thomas and Mina Edison shortly after they got married.

inventor and manufacturer. Mr. Miller was also one of the founders of the Chautauqua Institute, an organization that sponsored a series of lectures, concerts, and plays each summer.

Because they were so seldom alone, Edison taught Mina Morse code so they could send each other private messages by tapping them into each other's palms. He even proposed to her this way, and she responded by tapping "yes." Their wedding was set for the following February.

That winter, Edison and Gilliland traveled to southern Florida, where Edison was surprised to find an abundant supply of bamboo in the Everglades, a large wetland covering much of the southern part of the state. Both he and Gilliland liked Florida so much they purchased land in Fort Myers on the state's southwest coast, where they both planned to build winter homes.

When Edison returned to New Jersey, he purchased Glenmont, a

This is the living room on the second floor of Edison's Glenmont estate. Edison and his wife often spent evenings here playing the game Parcheesi.

twenty-nine-room mansion in Llewellyn for his new bride. He and Mina were married on February 24, 1886. After his marriage, Edison once again plunged into work, always juggling a multitude of projects. As Matthew Josephson, one of his biographers, said, "It is breath-taking even to attempt to follow him as he moves restlessly from one type of investigation to others wholly different."

A NEW LAB

Over the next few years Edison was busy supervising the building of a new lab complex on land he purchased in 1887 in West Orange, New Jersey, managing his many electrical companies, and dealing with several ongoing lawsuits concerning patent infringements. He also carried out new experiments, some of which included an improved phonograph, yet another new filament material for his lightbulb, and a new way to mine ore. Madeleine, the first of his and Mina's three children, was also born in 1888. Their second child, Charles, followed a year later.

This is Edison's library at his West Orange lab. Besides thousands of books, the library contains photographs of important moments in Edison's life and his certificates and awards. To the right of the desk, there is a marble statue called "Genius of Electricity," which Edison bought at the Paris Universal Exposition of 1889.

His new lab, ten times the size of Menlo Park, was the most complete industrial research lab in world at that time. Along with machine shops, engine rooms, a glass blowing shop, and a vacuum-pumping room, there were chemical and photographic labs and special rooms for testing electrical equipment. A library fit for a university held ten thousand books. Glass cases displayed minerals, chemicals, metals, ores, animal hair, hooves, teeth, insects, and more. Edison once told someone he "ordered everything from an elephant's hide to the eyeballs of a United States senator."

The staff at the new lab, which numbered approximately eighty to one hundred people, was made up of some of the men from Menlo Park, some who had worked with Edison at his Electric Lamp Company and other factories, and many new employees. There were experimenters (some of whom were young apprentices hoping to learn from the master of invention), machinists, draftsmen, engineers, a fireman, a blacksmith, steam fitters, carpenters, and general laborers, as well as clerks and secretaries. As in any large company, employees came and went, but as had happened at Menlo Park, at the heart of the lab was a core of loyal workers who remained for many years.

In the early years at Menlo Park, work assignments were informal, given to whoever might be available at the time. This changed during the work on the lighting project, though, when each project was assigned to a specific assistant. This team approach was refined even more at West Orange.

As he had before, Edison worked long hours and expected his workers to do the same. He worked alongside his employees and joined them in their practical jokes and occasional horseplay.

With his multiple business interests, Edison was no longer able to be actively involved in every aspect of every operation, but he continued to keep a handle on things by making daily rounds to check on each team's progress. One of his employees said that as a boss, Edison was always considerate and, instead of criticizing, made suggestions as how to make something work better. However, another employee said that Edison sometimes was capable of biting sarcasm or ridicule, and that at times became so angry that he made "the sparks fly." In spite of this, that same employee also said, "We were a happy family at the laboratory."

A NEW PHONOGRAPH

Edison's original cylinder phonograph had made him known around the world, but its popularity faded quickly because it made poor recordings and was clumsy to use. Although at the time Edison said he would refine it, he was always busy with other things.

Other inventors, however, had continued to experiment with the device. In 1885, Charles Tainter, working at Alexander Graham Bell's laboratory, developed a wax coating for the cylinder that improved its recording ability. The people from Bell's lab showed Tainter's innovation to Edison and suggested they work together, but in his usual competitive fashion, Edison refused. He felt the phonograph was his "baby," and that Bell had stolen it. If anyone was going to make a better one, it would be Edison—on his own.

He began working on his new phonograph at his New York lab and brought it with him to West Orange. After two years, he had developed his own wax cylinder and a sapphire needle instead of a metal one, and continued working on improvements. He reorganized his Speaking Phonograph Company, hiring his old friend Ezra Gilliland to run it. However it wasn't long before serious business disagreements between them led to lawsuits and the end of their long friendship. Edison, however, continued to work on the phonograph and succeeded in producing a commercially successful machine. He then decided to apply his phonograph experiments to another new project he and his associate, W. K. L. Dickson, had been working on—something even more startling than the phonograph had been.

Edison's Other Inventions

Edison created an enormous number of inventions during his lifetime, including the first mimeograph, or copying, machine, a new way to manufacture plate glass, the fluorescent lamp, the fluoroscope (an early x-ray machine), an air compressor, a miner's safety lamp, and color movies.

NINE

Successes
and Failures

In 1889, Edison's many different electrical enterprises were combined into the Edison General Electric Company, in which Edison was a major stockholder. A few years later, that company merged with Thomson-Houston, another electric company. The new company was called General Electric. Although he was member of the board of directors, Edison had little to do with day-to-day operations. He was not happy with the new arrangements and decided it was time for him to get out of the electric business. "I am going to do something now, so different and so much bigger than anything I've ever done before," he said, "that people will forget my name was ever connected to anything electrical."

EDISON'S FOLLY

Back in 1880, when Edison thought he needed large amounts of platinum for his incandescent light filament, he had devised a machine to separate minute amounts of ore from sand and rock. When he decided on a carbon filament and no longer needed the platinum, he tried using his ore separator to extract small amounts of otherwise unobtainable iron ore from crushed rock. His first experiments were not successful, but that didn't stop him. In 1889, he purchased several old iron mines in and around New Jersey. He established a plant in Ogden, New Jersey, where he planned to crush 6,000 tons of rock a day, then use his ore separator to pull the ore out.

Edison devoted a good part of ten years of his life to this project and poured millions of dollars into it, but it was nothing but trouble. He was plagued with breakdowns, accidents, and technical problems. For approximately five years he, together with his longtime assistants, William Dickson, Walter Mallory, and Charles Batchelor, spent most of their time at the plant. Many people called this venture "Edison's Folly." As usual, Edison refused to give up. Only after a new and cheap source of good ore was discovered in the western part of the country around 1900 did he admit defeat and close the operation.

EDISON THE MOVIE MOGUL

No one project ever took 100 percent of Edison's time. While much of his energy was devoted to his ill-fated ore project, he continued work on his updated phonograph and another new venture that grew out of a meeting he had with Eadweard Muybridge in the spring of 1888. Muybridge showed Edison a strip of photographs mounted on the rotating drum of a popular parlor toy of the day called a zoetrope, or wheel of life. The individual photos were very slight variations of a single subject, but when viewed through the little slots of the spinning drum, the photographs gave the illusion of movement.

Edison's brain whirred. He made a preliminary sketch of a machine that would "do for the eye what the phonograph does for the ear." He gave the sketch to Dickson, who was an accomplished photographer, and asked him to design a camera to record actual movement. Within a few months, Edison and Dickson filed a patent for what they called a kinetoscope. This was one of the few times another person's name was included on one of Edison's patents.

Edison's idea was to combine this new device with his phonograph to produce talking films. During the summer of 1889, Edison and Mina traveled to Europe. They visited the Paris Universal Exposition, where many of Edison's inventions were being featured. Then they traveled to England and Germany. When they returned home in the fall, Edison learned that George Eastman had developed a new, flexible, celluloid film and immediately ordered some. Edison devised a sprocket system for advancing the film in the camera. He then traveled to North Carolina to investigate the possibility of using his ore separator to retrieve gold ore locked in the veins of old mines there.

When Edison returned from North Carolina, Dickson took him to the lab. A large projector and a phonograph were set up in the back of the room. On the opposite wall was a large screen. Dickson darkened the room and turned a crank on his projector. On the screen appeared a fuzzy, jerky picture of Dickson raising his hat and saying, "Good morning, Mr.

Edison, glad to have you back. I hope you are satisfied with the kineto-graph," which is what he named the projector.

Dickson's test film used only a short burst of dialogue, but when the two men tried to synchronize sound with an entire film, it proved too much of a problem to be practical. Edison and Dickson were attempting something not yet technologically possible. They gave up the idea of using the phonograph in conjunction with the movie camera and worked on each as separate inventions. For a while, they also abandoned their efforts to project images onto a screen. Instead, Edison devised a small, closed box in which to view the images. The very first motion pictures were born.

Progress on their motion pictures moved slowly, as it was interrupted by Edison's and Dickson's frequent jaunts to Ogden to work on the ore project, but it did continue. In the fall of 1893, visitors to West Orange were puzzled by the strange new building being erected. Built on a pivot, the structure was oblong in shape, with a sloped, hinged roof that opened to the sunlight. Black tar paper covered the walls of a large, windowless room, which featured a stage draped in black cloth. Inside this strange building whirred Edison's first motion picture camera. Nicknamed "Black Maria" because it reminded people of the windowless police wagons that transported criminals, it was the world's first motion-picture studio.

Those early movies were produced on small loops of film perforated on either side. They ran over a sprocketed wheel turned by a small electric motor and were lit by an ordinary incandescent bulb inside a wooden box with a peephole on top. Edison added a coin slot to the machine and sold several of them to a group of investors who opened kinetoscope parlors in cities across the United States and in Europe. Lines of people waited patiently for their turn to drop a quarter—an hour's wage for many of them—into the slot and bend over the peephole for their sixteen-second show.

Once again, Edison proved himself an adept entrepreneur. His Kinetoscope Exhibition Company made him the world's first commercial movie producer. Most of his films featured staged prize fights, vaudeville, or circus acts.

Edison was happy with all the money he was making from his kinetoscopes. Dickson, however, wanted to work on movies projected onto a large screen to be shown in theaters, and he left Edison's employ. The novelty of the kinetoscope soon wore off, while large-screen projection became more popular. In 1896, Edison purchased rights for a large-screen projector designed by Thomas Armat. He then made his own version of the device and named it the Vitascope. Edison, Dickson, and Armat were not the only ones working on new movie inventions, and over the next several

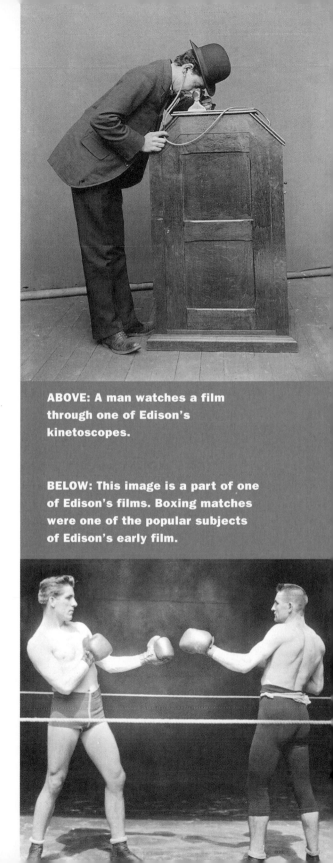

ABOVE: A man watches a film through one of Edison's kinetoscopes.

BELOW: This image is a part of one of Edison's films. Boxing matches were one of the popular subjects of Edison's early film.

years, there were lawsuits and countersuits claiming ownership of each improvement that was made.

Meanwhile, Edison's new family was growing. In 1898, his son Theodore, named for Mina's brother who had died in the Spanish American War, was born.

ANOTHER FAILURE

When Edison began working on films, he was engrossed in his ore project. When he finally gave up on that, around 1900, he wanted to find a way to recoup some of the enormous amounts of time, energy, and money he had invested. In order to use his ore separator, tons of rock first had to be crushed into sand. Sand is the basic ingredient in cement, so he decided to go into the cement business.

After inventing a new crushing machine and designing special kilns to make cement, he purchased land near Stewartsville, the center of the cement industry in New Jersey. Here he spent three and half years building a highly mechanized, modern plant. This project, like the ore, proved to be nothing but trouble. Delays, breakdowns in machinery, and difficulty producing the high-quality cement he wanted thwarted his efforts. One time, an explosion in the plant killed six workers and injured nine others. The plant closed down for repairs. Edison's financial advisors told him to close permanently, but Edison wouldn't listen.

He felt he could succeed with a new plan for making poured-concrete houses. This, too, was doomed to failure. His homes were too expensive, and no one was interested in purchasing them. Although some were built and still stand today, the idea was ahead of its time. Yankee Stadium in New

York was also built with Edison's poured concrete. Today, with more advanced technology, poured concrete is commonly used to mass-produce homes.

Edison was well known for his refusal to surrender to seemingly impossible odds. Sometimes this was a good thing, such as with his electric lighting plan. Sometimes, however, his tenacity was far beyond reasonable, and this was the case with both the ore and cement projects.

A NEW KIND OF BATTERY

The earliest automobiles, powered by steam, came out in the 1890s. By 1900, automobiles powered by gas, steam, and electric batteries were competing with each other. Edison felt electric cars would prevail over the others, if only they had an effective battery. Most batteries at that time were activated by lead and acid. The batteries were heavy and did not last very long. Edison designed a new type of battery that was smaller, lighter, cheaper, and longer lasting. His battery ran on an alkaline solution that was less corrosive than lead and acid.

Edison claimed his new battery would be trouble free and last indefinitely. Electric car owners rushed to buy Edison's batteries. Railroad owners installed them in their new electric engines. The success of the new batteries, however, was short lived. The batteries leaked. They lost their charge. The rubber molding around them cracked. Edison returned to his lab to fix the problems. After a year, he had made no progress. He had to recall the faulty batteries and close down his operation until he found the solution. He returned to the lab, where he conducted more than ten thousand experiments.

Despite some health challenges, Edison remained dedicated to his work.

By then, Edison was sixty years old. Although his health was beginning to decline, he worked as hard as ever. During the winter of 1905, work on all his projects came to a halt when he was rushed to the hospital for an emergency operation to remove a severe abscess from the mastoid bone in his ear. A few years later, he had a similar operation on the other ear. He had been partially deaf since early boyhood, but after his operations, he was almost totally deaf. That year, he was unable to take his annual Florida vacation. Once he recovered, he returned to working on his battery and other projects.

Edison spent seven years and close to $2 million working on his alkaline battery. Finally, on March 15, 1909, he noted in his lab book, "At last the battery is finished and all tests made except the jarring test which is being run now." The jarring tests consisted of driving a car 60 miles (97 km) over cobblestone streets and dropping batteries out of the lab's second- and third-story windows.

By then, though, gasoline-powered cars were becoming the only ones on the road. All was not lost, however. Edison's alkaline batteries were used in miner's lamps, railroad signals, in gun turrets on battleships, and in many other ways.

Robert Conot, one of Edison's biographers, wrote, "Edison had . . . given the battery industry almost as much of a push forward as he had the lighting industry . . . a generation before."

Automotive Industry in the Early 1900s

The first automobiles were produced at the end of the 1800s. By the early 1900s, more than 600,000 cars were owned in the United States. Some were run by steam, some by electric battery, and some by an internal combustion engine powered by gasoline. Steam-driven cars were easy to operate, but the engines were expensive to produce and maintain. Electric cars were quieter than steam, but once people began driving greater distances, the limited capacity of the battery made them impractical. Gas-powered cars became the standard.

At first, automobiles were produced in small, independent shops that had originally made bicycles, wagons, or various types of machinery. Then Henry Ford launched his assembly-line method of mass production in 1913 and quickly became the leading U.S. car maker. Henry Ford's Model T, introduced in 1908, quickly became the most popular car on the road. Edison designed an electric starter for Ford in 1912.

Edison stands by his son Charles, shortly after the organization of Thomas A. Edison, Inc. They are using one of Edison's inventions, the Ediphone.

TEN

A Most Productive Life

In 1904, when the lightbulb was twenty-five years old, the American Institute of Electrical Engineers threw a birthday party for Edison at which they named him America's most useful citizen. By this time, many people looked up to Edison as one of America's elder statesmen and philosophers. He enjoyed this and gave many interviews offering his opinions, not only on technology, but on family problems, women, clothing, diet, medicine, and education.

In 1911, Edison was sixty-four years old. Most men would have been thinking about retiring, but not Edison. He reorganized all of his companies into Thomas A. Edison, Incorporated (TAE) and continued working sixteen hours a day. He embarked on a new set of experiments to redesign his cylinder phonograph, which he still considered his special "baby," and had for many years provided income to help support his other businesses and endeavors. However, by the time TAE was formed, his cylinder design was facing stiff competition from the newer disc players, particularly those built by the Victor Talking Machine Company—the predecessor of the RCA Company. Consumers liked the Victor machine better because the records had a longer playing time, and the company offered recordings of classical music and opera performed by renowned artists.

As in the past, Edison couldn't stand the thought of being beaten by the competition, so he designed his own disc player and records. In his usual fashion, Edison was determined that his design would be better than that of his competitor's. He insisted that his machine and his records produce the highest possible sound quality, and in spite of his deafness, he insisted that he alone choose both the music and the artists who performed it.

Perhaps if he had not waited so long before offering a disc-type player, it would have been his machine instead of the Victor that became one of the best-known name in phonographs.

EDISON AND FORD

In 1897, Edison met a young engineer at the Detroit Edison Company. The young man was Henry Ford. Ford had long idolized Edison and was thrilled to meet him. He was even more thrilled when he told Edison about his plans to manufacture his own line of gasoline-powered cars and Edison encouraged him.

The two men did not meet again for sixteen years. By then, Ford's business was so successful that gas-powered cars had replaced both steam and electric ones. Ford asked Edison to design a self-starter for his cars to replace the hand crank then being used. Edison liked the younger man so much he invited him and his wife for a visit to his and Mina's winter home in Fort Myers, Florida. Ford then built his own winter home next door and the two families became close friends. Both Edison and Ford were interested in botany, and the two of them developed a huge experimental garden with plants of every description from all over the world.

FIRE DESTROYS THE WEST ORANGE LAB

In December of 1914, a fire broke out in Edison's West Orange lab. Due to the large amount of chemicals and celluloid film stored there, the fire raged uncontrollably. It was so hot that even the cement buildings Edison had built were destroyed. Watching the blaze with his son Charles, Edison said, "Where's Mother? Get her over here, and her friends, too. They'll never see a fire like this again."

Later that evening, he told Charles, "I am sixty-seven; but I'm not too old to make a fresh start." Within three weeks, the factories were rebuilt and his employees were back at work. Ford helped his good friend by giving him an interest-free loan of $750,000 to help offset the losses he had sustained.

Paul Israel, director of the Thomas A. Edison Papers Project at Rutgers University, and one of Edison's biographers, says, "Edison's response to the fire highlights a key element of his character. Where others might see disaster and failure he was always optimistically looking for opportunities and seeing the possibility of new directions for improvement." Israel points out that when Edison rebuilt his lab, he added many improvements to increase efficiency.

EDISON ENTERS GOVERNMENT

In 1915, Europe was embroiled in what became known as World War I, in which Germany attempted to conquer its neighbors. Before the war, Germany had been the world's leading supplier of industrial chemicals. Once the war began, these chemicals were no longer available to the United States or the European countries allied against Germany, so Edison's factories began manufacturing and selling industrial chemicals.

As it became clear that the United States would be drawn into the conflict, Edison and other scientists felt the United States should increase its technological preparedness. The Naval Consulting Board was established for this purpose, and Edison was named as its head. The United States joined European countries in the fight against Germany in 1917. Edison wanted the board to set up a scientific research laboratory for the United States Navy, but the board did not approve it. He also proposed several other things and submitted close to fifty new inventions for use by the navy, all of which Edison said were "perfectly good ones, but they were all pigeon-holed."

Although the Versailles Peace Treaty ended the war in 1918, the Naval Consulting Board remained in place. It wasn't until 1923 that the directing members voted to create the research lab, but by then Edison, angry because so many of his suggestions had not been accepted, had resigned his position.

Edison's health deteriorated as he entered his seventies. While he continued to work on his many different projects, he took more time off for vacations and spent more time at home with his wife. In 1926, he announced his retirement, saying he would continue to work, but only on his own laboratory experiments. His son Charles, who had worked with him for many years, took over as president of the company.

ANOTHER NEW VENTURE

Through his friendship with Henry Ford, Edison met Harvey Firestone, the founder of Firestone Tires. For several years, the three men took annual camping trips, driving across the country and sleeping under the stars. In 1915, the trio visited Luther Burbank's horticultural laboratory in

Edison and his friends relax during one of their yearly camping trips. This trip included Henry Ford, Edison, President Warren Harding, and Harvey Firestone. They were accompanied on their trips by a staff of cooks and attendants, reporters, and photographers.

California, where they discussed how the coming war would cause a crucial shortage of rubber. They also discussed the fact that since most of the rubber in the world came from Asian countries controlled by Great Britain, tire manufacturers in the United States were dependent on Great Britain's price controls. Perhaps, suggested his friends, Edison should find an alternative to Asian rubber.

Although Edison was eighty years old, he took up the challenge and began an intensive search for a rubber producing plant that grew in the United States. He wanted a plant that could be grown, harvested, and processed quickly. He read all he could about rubber. He sent for plant samples from every state. After studying more than seventeen thousand weeds, vines, shrubs, and trees, he decided that the common goldenrod plant was the best bet. By crossbreeding plants from several locations, he developed a plant that grew to 14 feet (4.3 m) and yielded 12 percent rubber. Mina said that during that period, "Everything turned to rubber in the

Edison (second from right) stands with his wife during the ceremony where he received the Congressional Medal of Honor.

family. We talked rubber, thought rubber, dreamed rubber." The goldenrod experiments petered out, though, as Edison's health declined. There is a story that Firestone's tire plant did manufacture four tires for Edison to use on one of the many cars supplied to him by Henry Ford, but these tires had been made from a different plant, not from goldenrod.

HONORS AND TRIBUTES

Edison received many honors during his lifetime, but two stood out above all the others. In 1928 he was awarded the Congressional Medal of Honor for the development and application of inventions that revolutionized civilization.

In October of 1929, Henry Ford and the General Electric Company co-hosted Light's Golden Jubilee, celebrating the fiftieth anniversary of the invention of the incandescent lightbulb, the start of the Electric Age, and Edison's lifetime of achievements.

The celebration was held at Greenfield Village, Ford's newly built museum in Dearborn, Michigan, as a tribute to the many accomplishments made by Americans during the 1800s.

For the Edison display, Ford purchased the decaying buildings of Menlo Park. When Edison, who was recovering from pneumonia and was still weak, arrived at Dearborn, Ford escorted him and Mina on a tour of his recreated Menlo Park. The old boardinghouse and Edison's farmhouse were there, and, of course, the lab—with its array of lighting-experiment equipment, dynamos, and assorted miscellany. Edison said, "Well, you've got this just about ninety-nine and one-half percent perfect—we never kept it as clean as this."

Along with the Menlo Park exhibit was a replica of the old Grand Trunk Railway, complete with Edison's baggage-car lab and a young news butcher selling the same sort of goods Edison had sold when he was a young boy. There was also a reproduction of his Fort Myers lab.

More than four hundred guests had been invited to this grand celebration, among whom were President Herbert Hoover, Marie Curie, Orville Wright, George Eastman, Harvey Firestone, Dr. Charles Mayo, Walter Chrysler, and John D. Rockefeller, Jr.

Edison and Ford rode the recreated Grand Trunk railroad to the Dearborn depot to meet President Hoover. On the ride back to Greenfield Village, Edison took the basket of fruit from the news butcher and sold a peach to President Hoover.

That night, Edison began his thank-you speech by saying, "I would be embarrassed at the honors that are being heaped upon me on this unforgettable night were it not for the fact that in honoring me you are also

Edison (seated), with his longtime friend Francis Jehl (far left), are about to re-enact the first lighting of the incandescent lamp at the Grand Jubilee Celebration put on for Edison by Henry Ford in 1929.

honoring that vast army of thinkers and workers of the past without whom my work would have gone for nothing." After his speech, Edison, exhausted, slumped in chair and was taken to his hotel.

Among the many accomplishments Edison was honored for were his telegraphy innovations, carbon-button telephone, phonograph, incandescent lightbulb and lighting system, and his movie camera. He was also remembered for his work in mining and cement, his many types of batteries, and his contributions to electric locomotive engines. In addition to his inventions, he had inadvertently set the stage for wireless radio and modern electronics, which are based on his etheric force and the Edison Effect.

After the Golden Jubilee, Edison returned home and continued to work despite his increasing weaknesses and bouts with illness. He filed what would be his last patent in January of 1931. That summer, he became very ill. On October 14, he lapsed into a coma. He died four days later on October 18.

A FINAL GOOD-BYE

Thousands of people lined up to view Edison's body at his West Orange lab. President Hoover and his wife, Calvin Coolidge, and Andrew Carnegie attended the funeral, as did many of Edison's former associates and employees.

As a final tribute to all Edison had given the world, from 10:00 P.M. to 10:02 P.M. on the evening of his funeral, lights were dimmed all across the United States, motion pictures stopped, the lights on Broadway were turned off, as were spotlights inside theaters, the torch on the Statue of Liberty was momentarily extinguished, and all subways in New York City stopped.

Timeline

THOMAS ALVA EDISON'S LIFE   WORLD EVENTS

1847 Edison is born on February 11 in Milan, Ohio.

1861 The U.S. Civil War begins.

1862 Edison gets his first telegraphy job in Port Huron.

The Battle of Shiloh takes place on April 6 and 7 in southern Tennessee.

1865 The U.S. Civil War ends.

1868 Edison files his first patent (vote recorder).

1869 Edison obtains a job at Law's Gold Indicator Co.

1870 Edison opens his first workshop, in Newark, New Jersey.

1871 Edison marries Mary Stilwell on December 25.

1873 Financial panic causes the U.S. stock market to be closed for ten days.

1876 Edison opens the Menlo Park lab.

1877 Edison invents the carbon-button telephone transmitter.

Edison invents the first cylinder phonograph.

1879 Edison achieves success with the incandescent lightbulb.

1881 Edison discovers the Edison Effect.

1884 Edison's first wife, Mary, dies on August 9.

1886 Edison marries Mina Miller on February 24.

1887 Edison establishes new factory and lab in West Orange, New Jersey.

1888 Edison and W. K. L. Dickson begin their work on the kinetoscope and kinetograph.

1889 Edison General Electric is formed.

1892 Edison General Electric merges with Thomson-Houston to become General Electric.

1893 "Black Maria" motion-picture studio is built.

1911 Edison's various companies merge into Thomas A. Edison, Inc.

1914 World War I begins.

1915 Edison is named head of the Naval Consulting Board

1918 World War I ends.

1926 Edison resigns as president of his company and becomes chairman of the board. His son Charles becomes president.

1928 Edison is awarded a Congressional Medal of Honor.

1931 Edison dies on October 18.

To Find Out More

BOOKS

Cousins, Margaret. *The Story of Thomas Alva Edison*. New York: Random House, 1997.

Cramer, Carol. *Thomas Edison*. Greenhaven Press, 2001.

Dolan, Ellen M. *Thomas Alva Edison: Inventor*. Berkeley Heights, NJ: Enslow, 1998

Delano, Marfe Ferguson. *Inventing the Future: A Photobiography of Thomas Alva Edison*. Washington, D.C: National Geographic, 2002.

Parker, Steve. *Thomas Edison and Electricity*. Broomall, PA: Chelsea House, 1995.

Sproul, Anna. *Thomas A. Edison: The Word's Greatest Inventor*. Blackbirch Press, 2000.

VIDEOS

Biography: Thomas Edison. A&E Home Video, 2000.

Edison: The Wizard of Light. A&E Home Video, 2000.

ORGANIZATIONS AND ONLINE SITES

Con Edison Energy Museum
145 East 14th Street
New York, NY 10011

This museum features exhibits on early electric lighting.

Early Recorded Sounds
http://www.tinfoil.com

You can hear early sound recordings made with two-minute wax cylinder records and old phonographs on this site. You can view vintage photos of early wax cylinders. Links are provided to other Edison sites.

Edison Birthplace Museum
9 Edison Drive
Milan, OH 44846
http://www.tomedison.org

This site has pictures of Edison's family home and furniture, Edison family memorabilia, and exhibits of Edison's inventions.

Edison-Ford Winter Estate Site
http://www.edison-ford-estate.com

This site provides information about Thomas Edison and Henry Ford and their estates in Fort Myers, Florida. It includes biographies, a photo tour, and audio and video clips.

Edison Home Page
http://www.thomasedison.com/

This site is mainly about the phonograph, but it also includes a list of his major inventions, Edison's writing about the phonograph, and sound files of early recordings.

Edison National Historic Site
Main St and Lakeside Ave
West Orange, NJ 07052
http://www.nps.gov/edis/home.htm

This National Park Service site provides information about and pictures of Edison's research lab, library, machine shop, chemical lab, a replica of the "Black Maria" movie studio, and demostrations of an early phonograph.

Edison's Papers at Rutgers University
http://edison.rutgers.edu

The Edison Papers project has catalogued and microfilmed original papers concerning Edison. The Web site provides access to most of these through a searchable database.

Henry Ford Museum and Greenfield Village
20900 Oakwood Blvd
Dearborn, MI 48121
http://www.hfmgv.org/

This site shows pictures of Menlo Park and tells about "Light's Golden Jubilee" that took place there in 1929.

Inventing Entertainment
http://memory.loc.gov/ammem/edhtml/edhome.html

This Library of Congress site provides a wealth of information on motion pictures and sound recordings of the Edison companies.

Menlo Park Memorial Tower and Menlo Park Museum
37 Christie Street
Edison, NJ 08820
http://www.edisonnj.org/menlopark/

This site provides information, photos, and sound. It also contains information about the museum and the 131-foot (39.9-m) tower topped with 14-foot (4.3-m)-high lightbulb on display there.

PBS—The American Experience
http://www.pbs.org/wgbh/amex/edison

This site includes the transcript of the 2000 television broadcast about Edison.

A Note on Sources

Researching this book was like embarking on a scavenger hunt. Each clue I found led me to another. To find the first clues, I searched the Internet for titles and authors of books about Edison. Then I went to the library. Because I live in a small town, my local library had only a few books about Edison, but the librarian helped me order all of the books I wanted through the Inter-Library Loan System (ILL). I then took the books home and read them. I used their bibliographies to help locate other books that I felt might be useful. I also used the Internet to find information from many of the sites I have listed in the To Find Out More section of this book. When using the Internet, make sure the site is one sponsored by a university, the government, or another reliable institution.

All the Web sites and books were helpful, but the one Web site that was most helpful was the Edison Papers at the Rutgers University site. This site allowed me to view hundreds of original documents. I looked at pages out of Edison's lab notebooks, newspaper articles written about Edison, and pages written by some of Edison's assistants and associates. Many of these were handwritten, as the typewriter had not yet been invented.

A few of the books I found most useful were *Edison: A Life of Invention,* by Paul Israel, the director of the Edison Papers site, *A Streak of Luck,* by Robert Conot, and *Edison: A Biography*, by Matthew Josephson.

There are many, many books about Edison. Some of the books contradict each other. Some of the books contain inaccurate information. One way of determining if information used by another researcher or biographer is accurate is to go back and read original information by the subject himself, or read the actual newspaper accounts instead of reading about those accounts. That is why the Edison Papers site is so valuable.

—Claire Price-Groff

Index

About the Author

Claire Price-Groff is the author of several books for young adults. She has written *Extraordinary Women Journalists* for Scholastic Library Publishing. Her other titles include *Twentieth Century Women Political Leaders*, *The Manatee*, *Great Conquerors*, *The Importance of Queen Elizabeth I*, and *Queen Victoria and Nineteenth Century England*. She especially enjoys writing about people who have helped to change the world. Ms. Price-Groff lives in the mountains of western North Carolina with her husband and their orange cat.